Friends for Life

Also by Jan Fennell

The Dog Listener
The Practical Dog Listener

Friends for Life

JAN FENNELL

Author of *The Dog Listener*

HarperCollins*Publishers*

HarperCollins*Publishers*
77–85 Fulham Palace Road,
Hammersmith, London W6 8JB

www.fireandwater.com

Copyright © Jan Fennell 2003
1 3 5 7 9 8 6 4 2

The Author asserts the moral right to
be identified as the author of this work

A catalogue record for this book is
available from the British Library

ISBN 0 00 715370 8

Set in Stempel Garamond by
Rowland Phototypesetting Ltd,
Bury St Edmunds, Suffolk

Printed in Great Britain by
Clays Ltd, St Ives plc

To all those who have helped make me
who I am

Contents

Acknowledgements

I thought that this would be the most difficult book to write, but putting my life into words helped me to find many answers. I know now how vital every event proved to be on my journey to become The Dog Listener.

Firstly, I would like to thank the Teams at Gillon Aitken and HarperCollins for their belief in me; especially my agent Mary Pachnos, who has been there for me every step of the way. She has become very dear to me.

More than ever I wish to acknowledge those who support me on a day to day basis. My partner Glenn Miller, who works tirelessly behind the scenes. Alison Powrie and my son Tony Knight who so proudly carry on my work world-wide, and Charlotte Medley who helps care for our wonderful pack. My family and friend who are always there for me. Together we have a lot of fun.

Jan F

Preface

The past decade has seen my life transformed in constantly surprising ways. Since I began developing my ideas about understanding the inner language of dogs, I have been granted experiences I would never have imagined possible.

It may sound strange, but as I have travelled around both the UK and other parts of the world, the most striking difference has been the interest people have taken in what I have to say. To appreciate how significant that is, you must understand that for much of my early life, the idea that anyone would be interested in anything I had to say was unthinkable to me. So the fact that people wanted not only to listen to my ideas but to go deeper and to know about the experiences that had led to their development took quite some getting used to, I can tell you.

From the outset, I noticed that a handful of questions recurred again and again. When and why did I fall in love with dogs? What made them so special? How did a Londoner like me end up living in rural Lincolnshire? How did I come to look for a better, kinder way of living with our best friends? What gave me the strength and conviction to persevere with those ideas when the world seemed full of people ready to knock them down? It never ceases to surprise me how curious people are to know these things.

As I began to tell the stories that provided the answers to such questions, new, even more unlikely ones arose. Was I going to turn those stories into a book? When was I going to write my memoirs? My response to these was a hearty, genuinely incredulous laugh. I simply dismissed the idea.

It was during the period I was completing my second book, *The Practical Dog Listener*, when I'd been asked about my early days for what seemed like the thousandth time, that I was forced to think again. I realized that perhaps, after all, I should write something that provided the answers to all these questions.

The result is this memoir, the story of my journey from London to rural Lincolnshire, from girlhood to motherhood, from ignorance to enlightenment – and occasionally, in all three cases, back again.

It has not been an easy undertaking. Subconsciously I know one of the reasons I put off doing this was a fear of awakening the ghosts of the past. On more than one occasion I was taken aback by the power and potency of the memories I revived.

The process of writing this book has confirmed several important things, however. One of them is that – for good or bad – I would not have reached the point I have in my life, without the experiences I have had. Nor would I have got here without the special friendships I have made along the way. There have been friends and family who have played their crucial parts. I have been blessed with two wonderful – at times inspirational – children. I hope I have done them all justice in the pages that follow.

Yet no one has made a greater contribution than the canine companions who have shared my life. I have known and loved so many of them over the years. They have come in all shapes and sizes, in every shade under the sun and from all manner of breeds and backgrounds. There have been short ones, shaggy ones, pedigree ones and some of deeply dubious parentage.

Since as far back as I can remember, dogs have been a constant in my life. From an early age growing up in the London of the 1950s, I was drawn to them like a magnet. Wherever I went a dog would appear. It was as if some irresistible natural force was pulling us together. Family and friends accepted it as a fact of life. Back then no one stopped to analyse why we formed such deep bonds, least of all me.

As a child, all I knew was that while other children felt wary and afraid of dogs, I somehow felt safer in their company. To me they were the most unthreatening creatures in the world, the most affectionate too, certainly more so than most humans. As my life moved on, I found nothing to alter that view.

Now I believe dogs hear voices we don't hear, possess senses we simply can't understand. They have an emotional sense so highly tuned it is beyond our understanding. Everyone who has ever lived with a dog knows what I mean. What else can explain the way that, at times when you are low emotionally, your dog always seems to be at your side? Dogs sense vulnerability and weakness. They have a gift for knowing when to provide the uncomplicated, unconditional companionship and love their human friends need.

It wasn't long after I set off on the voyage of self discovery that was the writing of this book, that I began to understand why, from the very start, dogs had played such a prominent role in my story. Now that journey is complete, I can see why they have remained friends for life.

Jan Fennell

Lincolnshire, January 2003

Chapter 1

Beautiful Girl

I was born of a loving relationship. The only problem was that where my mother and father were concerned, they reserved most of that love for each other. I was the only child, the little nuisance who got in the way, the living embodiment of the old saying that 'two's company but three's a crowd'. I often think I spent my childhood as an outsider looking in on their private happiness. I bear no resentment towards my parents. I have tried to understand how hard life was for them, and to a large degree I have succeeded. If I am brutally honest, however, there are still times when I ask myself why they bothered having me.

Until I came along, their story could have come straight off the pages of a slushy romantic novel. My mother, Nona Whitton, met my father, Wally Fennell, in London a year after the end of World War II, in 1946. It was a time of hardships, and the war still cast a long shadow over life in England.

My dad's war seemed like something out of Spike Milligan's madcap accounts of life in the Army. Dad always said 'war was a joke' and his experiences proved it. During his six years in the Army he was charged with desertion by one regiment when he was already fighting with another one altogether and reported dead when he was still very much alive.

The desertion charge was laid by the Royal Engineers, his second regiment, who called him up in 1941, two years into the war. They charged him when he failed to reply to his call-up papers, then discovered to their embarrassment that he had volunteered to serve with the Gloucesters when the war had first broken out.

Dad was a practical man and his talents suited the Royal Engineers. He was often sent behind enemy lines to prepare the way for the fighting divisions and it was during a mission somewhere in Europe, in 1943, that he was reported missing in action. The telegram that broke the news had a terrible effect on his father, George Fennell, who had already lost three of his six sons in tragic circumstances. The news that another was missing presumed dead was too much to bear. He died of a heart attack days later. My father never really forgave the Army for that; he had not been killed or captured at all and he turned up safe and well just in time to travel back to England for his father's funeral. What a happy homecoming that was for him.

My dad always believed in what he was fighting for, in serving King and Country. But he also believed war was a series of mishaps. Anybody whose job is to blow things up and then put them back together again doesn't feel very constructive in a war, he used to say. His philosophy seemed to have been that if you didn't laugh you'd go mad.

His nickname in the Army was 'Crash' because of all

the scrapes he got himself into. He was obviously a good soldier, being 'busted' as a sergeant, that is to say promoted then demoted again, seven times. His final promotion came in the field and was given by a Canadian officer who saw that my father was the one organizing everything. The officers didn't know what they were doing, according to my father; it was up to the ordinary enlisted men to sort out the mess the officers made.

The low point of my father's war came at Arnhem. His unit was moving forward with an escort of tanks into an area just recaptured from the Germans. They had been told the area was free of enemy troops and had been sent ahead to clear the path. No sooner had they set off than the German tanks came over the hill again and my dad was fleeing for cover.

It was a close-run thing, shells going off all over the place, men falling to the ground. Most of Dad's unit made it but when they reached safety in the trees someone said: 'Crash, look at your knee.' It was in bits. He had also badly damaged his elbow. But it wasn't the end of his war. The Army surgeons put his knee back together with a piece of silver wire. He went back to Europe and stayed on with the Royal Engineers, building bridges in post-war Holland until early 1946.

My father had been twenty-one when he left home. Six years later he returned from the war with a bad limp and the feeling that he had sacrificed his youth, his health and probably his chances of happiness. He often said the war took the best years of his life.

My mother, on the other hand, looked back on the war with feelings of nostalgia. I think the period between 1939 and 1945 provided her with the best time she ever had. For her life afterwards was an anticlimax.

Like my father, she was from west London. Without knowing the full details until much later I was aware that her childhood and teenage years had been tough. Her father had died relatively young, when her mother was expecting the fourth of their children. So when war broke out my mother, like many other young women, found it a liberating experience. She had a job working in a munitions factory, earned a good income and suddenly found herself part of a group of independent girlfriends who were determined to live every day and night as if it were their last – which in the London of the Blitz it might easily have been.

For Mum life was made all the more exciting by the fact that, at twenty, she was a really beautiful-looking girl. We never talked about that period much, for deeper reasons that would eventually reveal themselves. But I think she was engaged seven times. The one story Mum would recall, ad flippin' nauseam, was of the New Year's Eve party when Stewart Granger danced with her.

At the time he was one of the country's great matinée idols and everyone had been excited at the prospect of him coming to the party. He arrived late, close to midnight, and immediately announced he couldn't stay. 'I'm sorry I can't stop, but before I go I must dance with the most beautiful woman in the room,' he announced with a film star's sense of the theatrical. To Mum's delight he fixed his eyes on her, took her by the arm and whisked her around the dance floor. At the end of the dance he plonked a kiss on her – then bade her farewell. Well, that was the highlight of my mother's life, pretty much. Everybody who ever knew her knew about that. And it reinforced her view of how the world worked.

My mum, bless her, really believed that there was a crock of gold at the end of the rainbow. But her problem was that she never found the rainbow. Whenever it appeared it would vanish again abruptly, a little like Stewart Granger. She was one of those people who, having been told she was beautiful, didn't think she had to do anything else in life. She thought being beautiful was enough.

What she needed was someone to worship her. And in my father, she found the man to do it.

It was my father's sister-in-law, Elsie, who brought them together. She had worked with my mother at the munitions factory during the war. At work she had kept telling Nona that she must meet 'our Wally'. At home, she had kept telling my father he had to meet 'my Nona'.

When the war came to an end Elsie and Nona found jobs at a biscuit factory together. Elsie had just given birth to a baby boy and Nona had popped round to see her with a supply of free biscuits. Now my father came from a very musical family. He could play the ukulele, guitar, harmonica and concertina, but the day Nona visited he was playing the mandolin. She always remembered hearing it as she walked up to the door of Elsie and Uncle Bill's house. When she walked into the sitting room she saw my dad stretched out across a chair playing this beautiful instrument.

Violins might have been more appropriate. He said he looked at her and thought, 'I'm going to marry you.' Apparently she thought the same. He serenaded her into marriage.

My father truly believed that the stars had shone on him

when they brought my mother into his life. 'I'm so lucky to have her,' he would always say. She was, he discovered, a demanding woman. But from the outset he would do anything to make her happy.

My father worked as a driver. When I was a little girl he drove the No. 73 and the No. 11 bus through central London. By day he was a pretty ordinary guy, but by night he was transformed. He was a handsome man and in the evening he 'trod the boards', usually with his brother Bill. The brothers had inherited much of their talent from their father's family, who worked in Variety and could count Marie Lloyd as a family friend. In the family tradition they also mixed in a bit of vaudevillian playfulness. Their funniest sketch was something called 'The Ballsup Ballet', a spoof of the Bolshoi Ballet in which they dressed up in tutus. Singing, however, was their strong suit.

Dad had a wonderful voice. He would walk into a pub or a club and the shouts would go up straight away: 'Come on Wally, give us a song.' He used to do Bing Crosby and Maurice Chevalier numbers and had entertained dreams of making it as a professional singer. But when he had gone to see a West End agent he had been knocked back. 'There's already one Bing Crosby and we don't need another one,' he was told. Within a year a British singer called Michael Holliday, who Mum said was nowhere near as good as Dad let alone Bing Crosby, became a huge hit. That hurt Dad badly, I think.

During their courtship, Nona used to go to his concerts and he would sing a song from the musical *Singin' in the Rain* called 'Beautiful Girl'. I think it began: 'You're a gorgeous picture...' Such attention was music to my

6

mother's ears. She thought she'd finally found the crock of gold at the end of the rainbow. She fell hopelessly in love with him.

They were married in 1947. By the following year, I had joined them in the small upstairs flat they rented in Rosaline Road in Fulham, south-west London.

The Fulham I grew up in bears little resemblance to the trendy, cosmopolitan community it is today. One or two Greek shopkeepers apart, the area had few immigrants. The West Indian and Asian influxes of the late 1950s and 1960s had yet to happen.

Times were generally hard. Large parts of the area were rubble-strewn wastelands from the Blitz. We all lived in flats, most of them cramped. Ours consisted of a sitting room, a tiny kitchen, a toilet and one bedroom. It was the same when we moved to a home at the Clyde Flats on Rylston Road when I was three. For the first ten years of my life, my single bed was squeezed into a corner alongside my parents' double divan in a sleeping space ten feet square. Luxurious it wasn't. I understand now that those were difficult times. I also know a lot more about my parents' lives and the pressures they were under than I did then.

The war and its effects dominated everyone's life, of course. Rationing was still in existence, although if I'm honest, I was never aware of any real hardship in that sense. The most vivid reminder of the events of 1939 to 1945 lay out on the streets. You only had to walk outside our front door to see the damage the Blitz had inflicted. There were open bomb sites on almost every street in Fulham, including our own. As a child, of course, I had no concept of how these strange spaces had come to exist in the midst of such a built-up area. All I knew was they made great playgrounds.

For my generation the war was simply something that people banged on about a great deal. For the generation who had survived it, however, it had been a life-changing experience. And for men like my father the peace was almost a greater challenge. He found it hard readjusting to work. He had a succession of jobs, all of them involving driving but none of them well-paid by any stretch of the imagination. For my mother too, the end of the war brought her back to the grinding reality of life. By the time I was three or four she had left the factory for a clerical job with a wealthy local businessman, Sydney Smith.

They didn't have much money but they remained very social animals. Much of their amusement revolved around family – my father was one of eight children, my mother one of four, so there were lots of aunts and uncles around to visit. Everyone seemed to have a piano in their house. Singalongs and performances were very much part of the family's way of letting their hair down.

My father's music provided another escape from the daily grind. When I was three or four I was incorporated into the band my dad had now formed with Uncle Bill, his two kids, Maureen and Barry, and his older sister, Auntie Ivy, on piano. We used to do shows at old people's homes, village halls and places like that. I can remember travelling to suburbs like Pinner, though I can't recall how the act was billed.

We used to bring the house down with versions of things like 'Carolina in the Morning', 'Singin' in the Rain', 'Que Sera Sera' and a song called 'Get Out Get Under the Moon'.

Dad and Uncle Bill were good at slapstick too. They would pretend to be acrobats, but would deliberately mistime their stunts so that they continually bumped into each other. They also loved dressing up. Uncle Bill performed a black-face version of Al Jolson singing 'Mammy'. They also used to do a variation on the popular 'Egyptian Sand Dance' routine. They would dress up in costume for it, even putting on panstick colouring. I'll never forget the first time they did it. My father had gone to town on the make-up and he'd plastered his hair in Brylcreem and combed it down over the front of his face. He looked great, totally crazy. My mother was in the audience; she asked one of her friends: 'Who the hell is that?'

'It's your Wal, Nona,' she replied.

My mother nearly choked.

Our motto was to make them laugh, make them sing and make them cry occasionally too. It was my job to encourage the last of these in the routine that eventually became my major contribution to the show.

When he wanted to change the atmosphere my father used to sing a sentimental song called 'Daddy's Little Girl'. It was a lovely, lyrical song that showed Dad's voice off to the full. As he started singing it would be the cue for me to stand up in the audience, walk to the stage and sit there while he sang this tribute to me. Audiences loved it, naturally. It was tear-jerking stuff. If only I had felt as if I was Daddy's Little Girl.

Chapter 2

Family Values

It was inevitable that the first dog I called my own existed only in my imagination. My mother disliked animals intensely. As far as she was concerned dogs were messy, smelly creatures that moulted, left unpleasant odours and generally spoiled her spotless home. She had an uncanny ability to sense when I'd been within touching distance of a dog. It was as if she was equipped with a special radar. 'You've been playing with those dirty creatures again,' she'd scold me. If there was a golden rule in our home it was that my mother got her way. And so for the first fourteen years of my life, denied a dog of my own at home, I made friends with other people's pets – and made do with an imaginary one of my own.

I can still picture her now. She was a lovely, long-haired little thing, with huge, doe-like eyes. Whenever she saw me her ears would prick up, her tail would wag and her face would break into a broad smile. I sometimes wonder whether Walt Disney had adopted her as his own imaginary friend. She could have been drawn by him.

Sometimes I called her Lady, more often than not I

simply referred to her as My Little Dog. She used to appear whenever I felt hurt or lonely. As my childhood progressed, that meant she was an almost constant companion.

With my mum and dad it was always as if the world revolved around the two of them. I was filled with a sense that I somehow didn't fit into their plans – or indeed anyone else's.

We'd go to places then I'd be left sitting in a corner, with nobody to talk to. On holiday my mum would begin suggesting she and my dad should go off somewhere or other then say: 'Oh we can't, we've got Janice.' They'd always want me out from under their feet. I was a nuisance because I stopped their fun. I was always made to feel I was in the way.

Even within the family I felt left out. I had cousins, but because my dad was the second youngest of his brothers and sisters, they were all much older than me. I can remember watching them and envying the way they played with each other. It always seemed that there was no one for me, I was always the person on the outside looking in. Whenever there was a family do, my mum and dad would be together, my cousins would be together and I would be on the sidelines.

My mother's only interest in me lay in dressing me up.

Mum thought she wanted a child but what she really wanted, I believe, was a doll. She kitted me out in frilly, patterned dresses and fussed endlessly over my hair. I'm sure it pleased my mother that I was always being admired for my clothes or my hair; I had beautiful, tumbling ringlets. But to me it was a source of sadness that I was always admired for something else, never for myself.

So, from an early age, I had no choice but to make friendships elsewhere.

We used to spend a lot of time with my father's brother George. He had a dog called Rex, a lovely, gentle creature. Back in those days nobody had pedigrees, they had mutts. Rex was a mutt, a mixture of all sorts of influences. He was black and tan in colour, not very big; he had a curly tail, long pointy ears and a slightly foxy look. He probably had some German shepherd in him. But he was a hugely affectionate dog, and he loved directing that affection towards me.

He'd always make a beeline for me and fuss over me. I can recall how, whenever I arrived at their house on the edge of west London near Heathrow, Uncle George would say: 'Oh Rex, your friend's here.' Then, while the rest of the family were talking about their important lives, I'd sit stroking him or playing ball. It didn't stop me feeling something of an outsider within the family. But it did stop me feeling so lonely.

If my passion for animals had a source, it was inherited from my father's side of the family. My father liked animals himself. He had owned a dog called Gyp when he was younger and had worked with horses before the war. He used to say that he missed the old horse that pulled the cart on his bread round as a young lad in the 1930s. It had been replaced by a lorry. 'No matter how hard I whistled it wouldn't come to me like my old horse,' he would joke.

But it was my grandmother and my Great-Uncle Jim Fennell who really made an impression.

My paternal grandmother, Mary Ann Till, was a remarkable woman. She had grown up as part of a traditional travelling Romany family in the latter stages of the nineteenth century. Although she had said goodbye to that life a long time ago, she still wore a traditional Romany cap and smoked a pipe. She always seemed to have a cup of black, piping hot tea cradled in her hands. I can recall sitting on her knee listening to the tales she told of what, even then, seemed like a lost age.

Her parents toured the country making and selling lace and working as knife and blade makers. It was a seasonal life. The men spent the winter looking after the horses and making blades and the women made lace. Then when the spring came they would tour the stately homes of England.

The image of the wandering gypsy has always annoyed me. My grandmother recalls a life where they were welcomed by the well-to-do ladies of the manor, who would buy the lace while her father worked on all the knives and scythes.

Animals played an important part in their life. Horses and dogs were crucial members of the family business and were treated with respect. In fact, horses played their part in bringing my grandparents together.

When my great-grandparents died, the family wagon was burned according to the ceremonial traditions of the Romany nation. My grandmother and her sister were allowed to keep some of the family's possessions. But they themselves were passed on to another family for adoption. The sisters were deeply unhappy with their new family and kept running away. They never made it very far and were returned to the new family, where each time they were treated worse than before. Eventually their shoes were taken away from them to prevent them from breaking away again.

I didn't know my grandmother's sister very well, but I know my grandmother was a determined character. It was the middle of winter when they made their final, successful break for freedom. They found themselves outside London, in Middlesex, but they didn't know precisely where. They just ran, barefoot, carrying their few possessions bundled up. A blizzard was blowing and they were close to collapse when they stumbled across a horse-drawn cart on a pathway. Two young men, wrapped up in big coats, were driving the horse home through the snows. One of them shouted: 'Come on, girls, get up here.' The two men were my grandad, George Fennell and his brother, my Great-Uncle Jim. The pair ran a fruit and vegetable delivery business and had been out on their rounds when they were caught in the snow themselves. They were making sure the horse was looked after.

George and Jim took the two girls home to their parents; it turned out they had been lost in Hammersmith, then a village outside London. The girls stayed, and they and the brothers were eventually married.

My grandfather's family had an equally great respect for animals. My gran used to tell me a funny story about him. He had pulled up outside a pub, The Redan in Grafton Road, at the end of a working day. There were several horses and carts outside. My grandfather walked into the pub. Going up to one of the men at the bar, he asked him: 'Are you enjoying your beer?'

The man had hardly said yes when my grandad punched

14

him in the face. 'Go on, put a coat on your horse,' he said. 'You look after your horse first.'

They tended to hit first and ask questions afterwards back then. But the man hadn't put a coat and nosebag on his horse. My grandad was right – the animals were their livelihood.

Like many Romany women, Nan Fennell had the ability to foresee the future. She didn't always regard it as a positive attribute. Whenever anyone told her she had a wonderful gift she'd always say: 'It can be, but it can also be a terrible curse.'

It was easy to see why. Her family had suffered more than its fair share of tragedy. She foresaw the deaths of two children. The first was Uncle George's youngest, Ellen, the baby. Her older brother, the eldest of the grandchildren, was Johnny. When Ellen was born she was taken up to see my nan, who held Ellen in her arms for only a few moments before asking: 'Where's Johnny?' She was in a real state. 'Just get me Johnny.' When Johnny appeared, she said to him: 'We love you, and we always will, no matter what happens in your life.' The year after Nan died, Ellen was run over in a freak accident. Johnny was at the wheel of the lorry when it happened.

She foresaw tragedy again when her youngest son, Bill, and his wife Elsie had a son. When the baby boy, Trevor, was put in her arms all she said was: 'You love this baby, you make the most of this baby.' At the age of three the baby fell into the River Mole at Walton in Surrey and drowned.

On both occasions, people recalled my grandmother's words after the tragedies occurred. She didn't spell out what she had seen. Her philosophy was that you tell someone good news but you don't tell them bad. She had a happy knack of being able to tell her daughters and daughters-in-law that they were expecting babies – sometimes weeks before they'd even conceived. But on other occasions my father would just say: 'She's seen something.' She would see things then that would upset her deeply.

While I sat on my grandmother's lap, she would often tell me things. For instance, when I was six she predicted that I would have two children. 'But there will be more,' she said obliquely. It would be many years before that made any sense.

If Nan Fennell was a powerful force within the family, so too was my grandfather's brother, Jim, by far the most colourful of the clan. I remember vividly the day I finally summoned the courage to ask him about the awful lump he had on the back of his neck. How could I ever forget the story he told me?

As a thirteen-year-old boy growing up in Fulham at the end of the nineteenth century, Jim had headed off to see Buffalo Bill Cody's great Wild West show at Earls Court in 1896. He was so overwhelmed by what he saw that he went home that evening and promptly announced he was joining the show and heading off on their European tour.

He was the little boy who ran off with the circus – and a memorable time he had too. His experience working with horses stood him in good stead and he was put in charge of Buffalo Bill's stable.

Great-Uncle Jim was the family's natural performer, however, and he soon persuaded Buffalo Bill to give him a place in the show. While driving the famous Deadwood Stagecoach around the arena one night he was hit on the back of the neck by an Indian tomahawk. The blow was accidental but it split his neck wide open. 'That's where the hatchet hit me,' he told me.

It was Jim who introduced me to the first important animal in my life, his horse Kitty. Kitty was a typical Thelwell pony, as wide as she was tall, black with a long mane, her tail trailing down to the ground.

Great-Uncle Jim kept her in stables in Battersea Park, where he also kept the cart from which he sold his fruit and vegetables. I vividly remember Great-Uncle Jim placing me on her back and feeling the warmth and softness underneath me. Together we spent hours padding around Battersea on his horse and trap, talking about his adventures – and his love of horses.

Great-Uncle Jim had learned a lot from the native Americans he had worked with during his time with Buffalo Bill. He remembered one of them coming up to one of the horses one day before a performance, looking at it and saying: 'That horse is lame.' The cowboy who was due to ride the horse wasn't having any of it. 'To my shame I got the horse ready and let it go out into the arena. When it came back it broke down,' Uncle Jim told me. 'Bill Cody asked, "Didn't anybody spot it?"' Great-Uncle Jim said: 'He did,' and pointed to the native American.

Great-Uncle Jim had a huge respect for the quiet courage of those men. He disliked intensely the way they were presented as the 'baddies' in Buffalo Bill's show, in which the white men were always being rescued from the redskins. But from the stories he had heard the native Americans tell of their time back in the West, he wondered who needed rescuing from whom.

In that sense he was the first person who made me think about injustice. He gave me another important idea too.

His relationship with Kitty was almost telepathic. I remember Great-Uncle Jim used to be able to lay down the reins, put his arm around me and whisper a gentle, 'Take us home, Kit.' In London in those days there was hardly any traffic. Kitty would take her time going home at her own pace.

At the stables where he kept Kitty he would sit me on her, bareback, and tell me how important it was to become one with the horse, to become part of it. He didn't like the way 'the nobs', as he called them, used to ride, with a saddle and a whip. He would say: 'You must breathe at the same rate as it. Until you can take in every breath that it takes you've got nothing.' Again this was something he had picked up during his time with the native American horsemen.

Looking back on it now, I realize it was Great-Uncle Jim and Kitty who first instilled in me the idea of animals and humans working in harmony. As a little girl I saw them working together instinctively, as a team. There was no coercion, they understood each other perfectly. It seemed like the most natural thing in the world.

Chapter 3

A Secret Happiness

In 1951, as a three-year-old, my mum and dad took me to the Festival of Britain celebrations, just across the river in Battersea Park. The images of that day are burned indelibly into my memory.

I was too young to understand the wave of optimism the Festival had inspired. But I do vividly remember the sheer joy of the occasion. I remember my father and Uncle Fred were both wearing white shirts. In the sunshine they seemed dazzling – just like everything else in the park.

Battersea Park was filled with people. I recall the carousels and the candy floss, the sounds of the hurdy-gurdies and the fairground hucksters inviting people to 'Roll up, roll up'. But the thing that created the greatest impression was the little grey-white pony that was giving children rides in a special arena.

I immediately asked my parents for a ride. But, just as quickly, my mother made her opposition plain.

'You don't want to go on that nasty smelly thing,' she said. I was dressed in a smart new plaid dress, I remember. 'You don't want to ruin your nice dress.'

It was my Uncle Fred who conspired to help me. My mother wandered off at some point. I remember Uncle Fred bending down, beckoning to me and whispering. 'Come on, come on. Now's your chance,' he said.

I ran over to the pony arena with him. Before I knew it I was being lifted on board the beautiful grey-white pony.

I'd yet to meet Uncle Jim's Kitty so this was the first time I'd sat on a horse. I can still remember the pungent smell. It was lovely then and remains so to this day. Forget your Chanel No. 5. As I was led around the arena on horseback I remember feeling on top of the world. I felt like a princess, it was so special. I would have stayed there all day.

One of the attendants led the pony round in a slow circuit of the arena. As he took me back to where I'd started I saw my time was up. I could see my dad and Uncle Fred with big beaming smiles but behind them was my mother with a face like thunder.

'I thought I said she couldn't, Wal,' she snapped at my father as I was led away from the arena a few moments later. 'What's the point of putting her in nice clothes if they're going to smell of filthy animals?'

The incident confirmed something that was already becoming clear to me. There was a clear hierarchy in our house. And I was at the bottom of the pecking order.

My parents' attitude to children was a throwback to the Victorian era in many ways. I should be seen and not heard. My opinion wasn't of any importance to anyone. All that mattered, to my mother at least, was that I present a happy, polite, smiling face to the world. Unless, that is, she wanted to show off my singing and dancing abilities at a family gathering. Even then, the only words I got from her were chastisement if I hadn't done something to the standard she expected.

At the time this upset me deeply, but I no longer feel that way. I understand now that she was merely reflecting the values passed on to her. She and my father were trying to provide a better life for me than they had enjoyed themselves. But it was as if they had had me out of a sense of duty, and then resented the duty that came with it.

There was no doubt they gave me the best they could afford. They bought me lots of toys, for instance. But then they would spoil it by not allowing me to play with them because they got in the way and messed up my mum's house. I was only allowed to play with one toy at a time.

There was no point arguing about things like this. I was expected to accept that they did things for my own good. If I ever upset the apple cart, they'd say: 'After all I've done for you . . .' And if I protested too much, my mother was very quick to smack.

If I was at the bottom of the pecking order at home, my mother was very much at the top.

My father would literally wait on her hand and foot. He would say that he was so lucky to have her, he would do anything for her. He would protect her from being upset, even if it meant hiding the truth.

If anybody said anything she didn't like or upset her, the waterworks would start and she would just cry. He couldn't cope with that, he'd fall to pieces. Of course if I tried a similar tactic, it didn't work. They would tell me: 'We'll give you something to cry for.'

So when I started showing an interest in animals, I sensed

there would be problems from the beginning. Mum didn't like me being near them, it was as simple as that. To her it was more important that I look immaculate and well turned out. And animals didn't fit in with that.

As I have said, my mother's feelings always came first. She always got her own way. But she was asking too much in this instance. And fortunately there were members of the family who were willing to conspire with me.

It was my grandmothers who best understood the closeness of the bonds I was forming with animals.

The family had a number of dogs and by the time I was five or six I had formed a mutual admiration society with all of them. Wherever I went a dog would appear. My cousin Doreen, to whom I was very close, had a smashing dog called Tinker. He was ever so playful, a lovely long-coated creature, and I would spend endless hours playing with him. As a family we used to go on camping weekends to Walton in the Mole Valley. I recall there was a dog called Bunty in the tent next to our regular spot. My job was to go and get water from the standpipe but I always ended up playing with Bunty, a big shaggy dog like a mop. Playing with Bunty was the highlight of the weekend for me.

Nan Fennell knew how lonely and unhappy I was at home and encouraged me to cherish these new friendships. I will never forget what she said to me once. 'They are a part of your life that is magic, that is special,' she told me. 'No one can spoil that. When you have the love and trust of an animal, nobody can ever spoil it. That is your secret happiness.'

She also defended my love of animals in the face of my mother's hostility. Whenever my mother had a go at me

22

in her presence she used to say: 'She's got a love of animals. It's in her and it always will be, you can't change that.'

But it was my mother's mother who did most to conspire with me. Nan Whitton, as I knew her, lived nearby. She was a lady, in the very real sense of that word. She came from landed gentry in Northamptonshire but had become estranged from her family, the Thorneycrofts, after marrying a sailor named Edward Whitton. The family thought he was 'beneath her' and made no secret of it. Tragically he'd died during the flu epidemic of 1922 and she'd been left to fend for herself with four children. It was a tough life, yet despite the hardships she'd remained a dignified, gentle woman. I never once heard her swear or even lose her temper.

She had a real air about her. She was six foot tall and always immaculately turned out. She'd always dress up, even to go to the shops, putting on matching accessories and carrying an umbrella with a bow. Whenever I went out walking with her I'd see workmen doffing their caps to her as if she were a member of the aristocracy. She'd return the compliment with a gracious nod.

At home she'd spend hours doing embroidery and reading – something not many of my family did. I can also remember painstakingly polishing her silver with her.

This may well have been where my mother got her airs and graces from. But whatever their roots, Nan Whitton knew her daughter's moods better than anyone, so she provided me with a source of affection that was a real life-saver at times. 'I'm always here for a cuddle,' she'd say. And she saw how fond I was of her cat, Smokey.

Smokey, bless him, was the ugliest cat you've ever seen.

His head was lop-sided. He was a big black moggy. Yet that cat was so affectionate. He had a purr like a traction engine. I lay on the landing looking at Smokey one day. Nan was in the kitchen. I said to her: 'Why do you love Smokey?' I was confused because my mum used to tell me you could only be loved if you were beautiful, that ugly didn't get loved.

My nan looked out of the kitchen and said: 'Only me and his mother could love him.' To her the fact that he was ugly didn't matter. To her 'beautiful is as beautiful does'. It was a thought that would have been lost on my mother. But it made a big impression on me. Mum didn't like me playing with Smokey, of course. I'd try like mad to brush the hairs off but as soon as I took one step into the flat she'd say: 'You've been near that cat again.'

So Nan Whitton taught me to carry two cardigans with me. I always used to have a little bucket bag in which I put a spare cardigan. I used to wear one while I was with the dogs or cats then change over. I would take the cardigan covered in hairs around to Nan Whitton. She must have been a magician, because somehow she always got the hairs off.

And it was she who helped me spend time with Digger, the first dog I really considered my own.

Digger belonged to our friends Peggy and Eddie, who lived in East Molesey. He was a little sandy-coloured Cairn terrier, a great little dog, hardy and a lot of fun. He and I got on like a house on fire. Whenever I went there, he was as pleased to see me as I was to see him. He would be up on his hind legs. He was my boy. He was there for me. Every time I looked at him or spoke to him his tail wagged.

With Digger, as with all the dogs I met at the time, I felt there were no conditions, I could be myself rather than the person that other people wanted me to be. He didn't make me feel as if I was in the way.

I was so fond of Digger that I went to great lengths to orchestrate time with him.

Once I feigned sleep in order to stay the night at the house rather than go back to Fulham. I lay on a sofa with my eyes closed and heard my dad saying: 'She's exhausted.'

My mum said he should carry me out to the car. Finally Peggy said: 'Oh, let her sleep here the night, we'll run her back tomorrow.'

I thought: 'Yes.' Isn't that pathetic?

I had to go along with the charade now and it was very odd lying there as my dad carried me up to a strange bedroom. Of course, as soon as the house was quiet I slipped down to give my canine pal a cuddle and I was up at the crack of dawn the next morning playing with him.

It was during a summer holiday that Nan Whitton helped me to effectively adopt Digger. Uncle Eddie used to work in Munster Road in Fulham where he had a workshop. Every day I went round to collect Digger from him, then took him to my nan's house. Of course my mother knew nothing about this. It only lasted a few weeks but I still look back on it as a great time.

My secret friendship with Digger taught me much. Being with him seemed to change the world around me. Confined within my mother's world no one spoke to me. Out walking Digger that summer I found people stopping for no apparent reason and talking away to me. I saw that dogs were great icebreakers.

I can remember how people used to tell me stories about their dogs. I could see the happiness they brought into their lives. By the end of the holiday, my nan and I had our own favourite memories of our time with Digger; we nicknamed him Digger Doughnut because of his love of the buns we'd slip under the tables of cafeterias we visited together during that long summer.

It only strengthened my determination to form more lasting friendships like this.

My mum had her secrets too, hidden parts of her life that only increased the distance between us. It was while we were out shopping one day around this time that I got a glimpse of a darker and more dangerous aspect to her life.

Shopping was the one subject my mother was happy to talk to me about. Her love of clothes was great. And it formed the centrepiece of our weekly expeditions down the North End Road.

We would start with a meal at Manzi's, the famous eel and pie shop. I would have pie, mash and liquor, she would have eels, mash and liquor. Then we'd head off to pick up the week's provisions at the local stores. My mother would always look in Madam Lee's fashion house. She'd spend what seemed like hours there, looking at things and trying them on. She'd ask the proprietor to put things by for her until the following week. She bought a lot from there. When we'd finished our expedition we'd head to Dawes Road and a bus back home, laden with shopping.

While we were waiting for the bus home one day I became aware that my mother was angry. We had seen two large men walk by us and head into a doorway. As they had done so they had recognized my mother and said something to her.

I knew who they must be, but – as I had been taught – I said nothing.

The London of the 1960s was run by gangs. Fulham's leading gangster was Charlie Mitchell, or King Charles as he was known locally. The men who worked for Mitchell were enormous gorillas; their hands looked like bunches of bananas. Bits of their ears were missing, they were gruesome. But you didn't ask questions. That's what I was always told: 'Don't open your mouth, their business is their business.'

My mother's connections with Charlie Mitchell were shadowy but I knew they were mainly through her brother George, who was his book-keeper. Mitchell had a number of legitimate businesses – things like money lending and bookmaking – and George looked after the books for him.

I would continue to be given glimpses into this murky world in the years that followed. A friend of my Uncle George, Mickey Salmon – Mickey the Fish – took a dive for Charlie Mitchell for dog doping. He came out of prison when I was about fourteen, and we all went to a club for a party for him. Prison hadn't been good to him; he looked terrible. It was a private party and I remember the owner asking me to fetch some glasses. I went over to a table and I can recall a man with terrifying eyes looking at me, smiling and saying: 'Hello, love.' I replied: 'Thank you.' When I asked my Uncle George who they were, he just said: 'You keep away from them, just keep away.' It turned out to be one of the Kray twins.

After Uncle George died unexpectedly in his early fifties, leaving his second wife and their four young children, my mother went to see his widow and asked her if she was going to be OK. She just told my mum to go upstairs. My mother went up to the bedroom and found rolls of money strewn on the bed, hundreds and hundreds of pounds.

It was George who was at the root of her anger that day, it turned out. Being a child I only heard part of the story, but I do know that my Uncle George's personal life was a bit of a problem. He used to take off every now and again, just disappear. He would take time out.

It seems that on this occasion the rumour was going around that Uncle George had absconded with some of Charlie Mitchell's money. It was absolutely untrue but the situation was complicated by the fact that Mitchell's colleagues needed George's signature to actually get to their money. So for a while all their businesses were tied up.

The two men my mother had seen that day worked for Mitchell. Something they said to her must have set her off, because suddenly she grabbed me by the arms and said: 'I've had enough of this.'

Charlie Mitchell's main offices were right opposite the bus stop. She went through the front door and barged straight in. There were five huge guys around a desk. My mum said: 'Now look, I've had enough of this, my George is as straight as the day is long and you know that. Any more of these lies and I will bring the law into this office, I know enough to have you put behind bars.' I stood there and thought to myself, 'What's she doing? She's lost her mind.'

I was thinking, 'Someone's going to pull a gun.'

Charlie Mitchell sat behind the desk. He was scary. Instead of standing up and threatening her, however, the mood was conciliatory. Mitchell said: 'Nona, come on, sit down, let's talk about this.'

But my mother was having none of it. She stood up with her shopping and stormed out again, leaving me in the room. It was only when she got to the bottom of the steps that she shouted: 'Janice, come on.' I was still shaking when we got home that night.

Looking back, it was a terrifying yet intensely revealing moment in my young life. It showed me a woman I had never seen before.

She loved her baby brother and was prepared to go to any lengths to protect him. In some ways I admired her for doing that. Yet in others it made her seem an even more distant, almost unknowable figure. I felt I knew her less well than ever.

It was the one and only time I came across Charlie Mitchell. Not long after that incident he survived an attempted shooting in Stevenage Road, near Fulham Football Club. Some time afterwards, like so many of London's gangsters, he fled to Spain and the so-called Costa Del Crime. His exile in the sun didn't get him far enough away from his enemies, however. He was shot dead there in the 1970s.

Chapter 4

Arrivals

At the age of five I began attending the local school, Sherbrooke Road Junior. It was little wonder I didn't warm to the place. From the very beginning, it had painful connotations for me.

I had been looking forward to starting school for one reason: my cousin Les was due to start at the same time.

I had come to know and love Les when my mother returned to work. Mum's absence meant I spent most of my time at Nan Whitton's flat in Alistree Road. For the first time I got to know her niece Joan and her son Les, who lived on the second floor of the same block.

Les was two months younger than me. His father, Uncle Alex, was an ex-Army man and very strict and austere. We weren't allowed to play together often, but when we did we really got on like a house on fire. He was as close as I had to a brother and I treated him with all the affection I would have shown a brother.

I can remember that in the run-up to my first term, Les and I had heard a lot of talk about us starting school. We both fully expected not just to be in the same school but in the same class.

On the first morning of term we discovered our parents had made other plans. I was being walked to school by Nan Whitton while Les was being taken by his mother, Aunt Joan. I have a memory of the two of us skipping along, tugging excitedly at the adults' arms, hardly able to contain our excitement at getting to the school gates. Our mood changed when we reached a zebra crossing on Munster Road.

'Say goodbye to your cousin Les,' my nan said to me.

'Why?' I replied, baffled.

'He's going to a different school to you,' she explained.

I was devastated, as he was. We both started crying. As he headed off in one direction and I went in another, we were both tugging again, but for different reasons. I can still see Les looking back at me, tears in his eyes.

It was only in the ensuing years that I learned what had happened. Les's father Alex had very clear ideas about what he expected for his son. From the beginning the family had plans for him. He was to study hard and go to university. He was to get a profession and get on in the world.

When he and I had reached school age, it had apparently been decided that it was 'for the best' if we were separated. Basically I was considered a 'bad influence' by Uncle Alex and Aunt Joan. Apart from anything else, I was a girl, and the family's expectations for me were zero. This could only mean that I would be a distraction for Les. So while he was put down for the better school in the area at Munster Road, I was to be sent to Sherbrooke Road.

31

My early memories of Sherbrooke Road school are dominated by that moment. All I can remember feeling is a mixture of anger and confusion. I felt as if Les had been taken away from me.

I fitted into my class well enough. The teacher, a Welsh lady called Miss Davies, took a bit of a shine to me and treated me well. But, if I'm honest, my heart wasn't really in it. I made few friends, probably because I was afraid of losing them like I'd lost Les. I settled into the routine of being an average student in an average school. I began fulfilling my family's expectations of me by achieving precisely nothing.

As I set off on what was to be an unhappy school life, the one consolation was that my parents' resistance to my having a pet had finally begun to crumble. My father in particular sensed my desperation. I think he knew I needed something living and breathing to take care of and to keep me company at the same time. So it was that he and my mother agreed to get me my first pet, a hamster, which I called Bimbo. His brief stay with us set the precedent for what was to become a depressingly familiar pattern over the following years.

Mum had only agreed to the hamster on strict conditions. She really objected to the mess, so it was Dad's job to clear up. It was soon clear that Mum's requirements were more important than mine. My parents hadn't thought that hamsters are nocturnal creatures. So Bimbo would sleep all day then come out to play when I went to bed. I barely saw him. At the time, of course, I wondered whether this was deliberate but there was no point in my complaining. 'You've got a pet, what's the matter with you?' I'd be told in no uncertain terms.

As it turned out, it didn't really matter. One evening my mother decided she should get to know Bimbo a little better. I have no idea why she did this. She hadn't shown much interest in him until now. And she approached the cage with gritted teeth.

Animals sense things and Bimbo, it seems, sensed my mother's disdain. So he nipped her on the finger. I can still remember the yell. Before I knew it, Bimbo had been banished to school. My father had a word with the headmistress and so Bimbo became the school's hamster.

This only served to make my sense of loss even worse, of course. It wasn't just that I could see him in his cage every day at school. Every weekend and holiday a child had a turn in taking him home. Every child, that was, except me. I wasn't allowed to take him home.

It is only now, looking back on that time, that I realize just how desperate and pathetic my desire for company must have looked to other people. Soon after Bimbo's departure I headed off, in cahoots with a friend of mine called Eric, to the graveyard at the local Catholic church, St Thomas's across Escort Road. Armed with a bucket, Eric and I snuck around the gravestones scraping off snails and had soon collected hundreds.

I took them home. I hadn't thought about where I was going to keep them, I had only thought to myself that I had some pets. I seem to remember I had even started giving each of them names. My hopes were soon dashed, though. I got to the front door and my mother opened it. She just screamed.

She went absolutely mad. 'Get rid of them, don't you dare bring them into my home!' On reflection, slimy snails are not the most natural domestic pets, but that's how desperate I was.

So I had to take them back to the churchyard. I can remember tipping the bucket and the snails just sticking there. They wouldn't budge. Suddenly I heard a voice behind me: 'Can I help you?' It was the priest. I was ever so scared. 'I think we can help them on their way,' he said and he took me and the bucket over to a tap where we poured some water in. He was ever so gentle and kind. And he tipped them out into the grass.

'One day you'll have a pet of your own,' he said.

'One day I'll have hundreds,' I said with a trembling lip.

Perhaps inspired by the snails, my father's next gift to me was two tadpoles, Alfie and Georgie, as I had soon christened them. Again my mother had accepted this under extreme duress. She let me use one of her best fruit bowls, a boat-shaped glass affair, as Alfie and Georgie's home. I can still see the constant pained expression she wore whenever she passed anywhere near them. It was saying: 'Do I have to have this in my living room?'

She must have been quietly delighted that their stay was so brief. Once more, things hadn't been very well thought out. Georgie died just as he was metamorphosing into a frog. His tail had begun to shrink, some rear legs had grown and a set of front legs had begun to develop too. Then Alfie died at the same stage. We didn't realize they needed

34

a pond. It had been another disaster and I sobbed and sobbed and sobbed. Especially when I found out my dad had flushed them down the toilet.

When my father suggested a budgie, I thought my wait for a proper companion was finally over. The green hen bird he brought home, Bobo, quickly reduced my mother to a state of nervous agitation, however. Bobo wasn't the friendliest of creatures, it turned out. Every night she'd be allowed out to fly around for a while, with my mother following her around sweeping up wherever the bird had been. She was petrified of Bobo defecating on her best china, I think.

Their relationship was clearly doomed. And it came to a head one evening, in unforgettable circumstances.

I can still see the scene. Dad was in the kitchen and Mum was in the living room in front of the mirror getting herself ready to go out, which was a regular sight. She was putting on her make-up and Bobo – out of his cage for his evening exercise – was sitting on top of the mirror. To this day I don't know why, but all of a sudden Bobo flew down and got hold of my mother's lip.

Pandemonium broke out. My mother screamed in agony then started leaping and running around the room with Bobo swinging and flapping as she clung on to her lip. Blood gushed and furniture was sent crashing over. My father came flying into the room shouting. 'Stand still, Nona!' Eventually he prised the bird free, leaving my mother sobbing uncontrollably. Luckily the damage was only cosmetic, although – naturally – my mother failed to appreciate that.

Throughout it all I sat there, consumed by what I knew

would be the inevitable consequence of what was occurring. I kept thinking: 'Bye bye, Bobo.'

Bobo went next door to the neighbours, who had their own budgie, Pippa. When they bred I persuaded my dad to let me have one of the babies, a tiny lump of fluffy blue.

It took some doing, I can tell you. My mother, of course, was adamant that it would have to have a cage large enough to exercise in and could never be left free to fly around and wreak the kind of mayhem poor Bobo had inflicted. We agreed.

But as it turned out, Bluey, as the new arrival was christened, turned into my mother's personal favourite.

He was an absolute character, a real gold-plated star. He used to talk to me in the morning; he'd say: 'Janice, come on, get up.' He'd recite nursery rhymes but say them upside down. 'Hickory dickory dock, up the Queen', was one of his favourites. He would dive into the lettuce bowl. What a character he was. My mother loved him, she was absolutely besotted by him, probably because he lavished so much attention on her. He'd say, 'Oh, you're beautiful,' and she loved that. Mum even deigned to let him fly around the house in the evenings.

We used to take him everywhere we went. He even came camping with us. I remember we once stayed next door to a family who had a bird called Bobby. One day the two birds were out in their cages and we heard ours talking. My mother's face turned scarlet when she heard her bird say: 'Bobby's a bugger, Bluey's beautiful.' We all burst out laughing. That bird was the light of our lives.

The time we had with Bluey was wonderful to me. To

be honest, despite all my love for animals, until then I hadn't realized an animal could be so loving in return. And the fact that he was the first successful pet I'd had made me love him back even more.

I was about to let Bluey out of his cage one November night in 1958, when there was a knock on the door. I opened it to discover a couple standing on the landing outside. They were an odd-looking pair: she looked nervous and was quite clearly heavily pregnant, he was a cocky young man in his twenties with the biggest Teddy Boy quiff I had ever seen. Whenever I see Woody Woodpecker I remember him.

'Is your mum in?' he asked.

I went to the sitting room to get Mum and was surprised when she recognized the Teddy Boy.

'Oh, hello, Ron,' she said, seemingly quite pleased to see him.

'Hello, this is my wife, Anne,' he replied, gesturing to the woman.

My mother ushered them into the sitting room and I, well-trained young girl that I was, headed to the kitchen to put the kettle on for a cup of tea.

I had been there for a minute or two when my mother reappeared. We didn't get many visitors at that time of the night. They weren't encouraged. Yet she seemed almost excited that these strangers had turned up out of the blue. I, on the other hand, had a dozen questions flying around my head. I only got to ask one, however.

'Who's that?' I said.

'That's your brother,' Mum replied breezily.

I'd always dreamt of having a brother or sister. I used to look enviously at my cousins playing, fighting and doing all the normal things siblings do together. I saw that when one got told off there would be huddles and muttered secrets would be shared. They were together.

But there was no prospect of me having one. Cousin Les had been the closest I'd had to a relative of my own age, but since our separation for school I'd seen less and less of him. Whenever I asked my parents, 'Can we have a baby?' they replied, 'No, we can't afford one.' And that was it, end of story. There was no discussion after that.

So to say the discovery that I already had a brother was a bombshell would be the understatement of the century. As my mother rushed back into the living room that night, I felt as if I'd been punched in the head.

The strange disorientation I felt was increased by the fact that my 'brother' seemed such an unlikely candidate to be my mother's son. I could hear him laughing in the sitting room. He was very loud and he spoke in a strong London accent. He was the sort of person my mother would normally have crossed the road to avoid. 'Common' would have been the word she used, most likely.

Eventually I took the tea tray in, but I might as well have been invisible. Anne was quiet because she'd just met her in-laws. I just sat on the floor listening, trying to take in what was going on.

I don't know whether I was pleased or hurt. In truth, I didn't know what I felt.

He'd say things like: 'I remember you when you were a snotty-nosed kid.' But that didn't add up. I had no memory of him at all. And besides, if I had a cold my family had the fastest hankies in town.

They backed him up though. They kept saying: 'You've met him before, you know Ron.' And I thought: 'No, I haven't. When? Where?'

There was no helping me to come to terms with the situation. There were no child psychologists around then to tell them 'This is a traumatic occasion for a child, a major event in her life, and you should proceed this way . . .' You just had to get on with it.

As I sat there listening it dawned on me that he was indeed my mother's son. He was calling my mother Mum and my father Wal. The only thing I could focus on that night was Anne's bump. I was thinking, young as I was, 'Maybe there's hope there.' I thought, 'I'm going to be an auntie.' Which would possibly give me a chance to be close to another human being.

I wasn't allowed to hang around for long. They obviously had important things to talk about, so I was sent to bed. I lay there in my bed with the door partially open. I can remember looking at the pattern that the paraffin heater left on the ceiling.

I heard them laughing. And eventually I heard them go, full of 'See you soon' and 'Pop round anytime'.

I went to school the next day telling everyone I had a brother. They did what they'd done when I said I had an uncle who worked with Buffalo Bill. They called me a liar again.

The aftershocks of that night continued for days and weeks. I couldn't help myself asking my mother questions. Who had she been married to? Where was he now? Why had she and Ron been separated? My mother really didn't want to discuss any of it. She'd get cross whenever I raised the subject. Divorce was not the done thing at that time and she clearly felt shame. A week or so after Ron had called round she snapped. I'd asked her another question about her divorce.

'I don't know why it's only me you're pestering with all your questions,' she said. 'Your father was married before too.'

This was another bolt from the blue. At least when I asked my father about it he was willing to talk to me. I sensed that he'd been expecting the question. He just sighed, shrugged his shoulders and said: 'Well, it was just one of those things love, there's not much to say really.'

It turned out that he had married before he'd gone off to war. His wife's name was Doris and she was a local girl. While my father was being blown to pieces in Europe, Doris did what a lot of young girls did and started becoming a little too familiar with some of the American GIs who were stationed in and around London. It had been when my dad came home for his father's funeral that he had discovered what she was up to. As if the pain of having to come home to bury his father hadn't been traumatic enough for him, he had walked into their home and caught her in flagrante. After the funeral he'd gone straight to the servicemen's charity, SAAFA, and asked them to organize a divorce. It wasn't particularly unusual for something like that to happen during the war, particularly to couples as young as my dad and Doris. They were both nineteen or so. But it still hit him hard. Looking back on it now it explained a lot about my father. It explained why he decided to stay on in Europe after the end of the war. He obviously didn't want to come home to be reminded of his heartache. It also explained why, having been given a second chance with my mother, he was absolutely determined not to let history repeat itself. No wonder he made her the centre of his universe, no wonder he rarely took his eyes off her.

My father's story was sad, but my mother's turned out to be even more poignant. It was many years before I got to know the full story. There were questions I needed to ask my mother when I became a mother myself. It was then that, slowly, she revealed what had happened.

It turned out that my mum had been just sixteen when she'd had Ron. The father was a local boy of the same age, Dan Godbeer. Mum told me she had been so naive she didn't even know she was pregnant. She didn't know the facts of life. She got married two days before he was born. The marriage didn't last, however. Dan went back to live with his mum and dad, my mum went back to live with her sister and her mother. Dan's mother was a poisonous woman and was determined to keep the baby in her family. The case went to court and the judge sided with her, saying in essence that a little boy couldn't be brought up by three women living in the poor, cramped conditions my mum and grandmother had to cope with. So Ron was taken from her.

The loss was terrible, but it was made even more painful by the fact that she would see him regularly. And when she did he was always dirty and badly dressed, sometimes in clothes that were one step removed from rags. Sometimes he was barefoot. She would spend ages making clothes for him and would then leave them in parcels on her mother-in-law's doorstep. But the packages would be sent back to her unopened. She was rejected. When he was about seven she gave up. She said it was the war that changed it for her. She adopted the same attitude as everyone else: 'We're going to die, let's make the most of the time we've got left.'

The story never came out in its entirety. I was given bits and pieces, which I had to put together. I eventually learned that it was my nan who reunited them. Sadly for Ron his father died when he was just nineteen. My dad took my mum to the funeral, but Ron didn't want to know her because he felt she'd abandoned him. Ron had joined the RAF as soon as he was old enough and my nan, bless her, invited him round for tea, because he was still in touch with her. She engineered it so that my mum would be there too, locked them in a room and said: 'Talk to each other.'

This, apparently, was soon after I was born. But I knew nothing of it. Even then, sadly, Ron fought against it. His grandmother was still bitter and made sure he thought the worst of my mother. But, as so often happens, when he was about to become a parent himself for the first time he finally came back. That strange, bewildering night in November 1958 was their reconciliation.

Again, with the benefit of hindsight I can see that it would have been a hugely significant night in my mother's life. I can only guess at some of the emotions she must have been feeling. But I can see how it must have affected her relationship with me. Her coldness, her distance from me, was perhaps her way of insulating herself from the pain of suffering a loss again. Maybe she daren't form too close a bond with me for fear of losing me too. It would also explain her possessiveness and over-controlling nature. She didn't want me to run away. And I can see now why she was so determined to dress me well and keep me immaculate at all times. She was not going to have me walking around the way her son had done. Part of me wonders, too, whether she felt angry still and took some of that out on me. Who knows?

Time has allowed me to realize why she reacted to Ron's reappearance in her life the way she did. In the immediate aftermath of that night, I watched her unleash all her money and affection on Ron, Anne and the new baby, David. Almost the next day she went out and bought Anne a lovely expensive necklace. When the baby arrived, they moved in near us. I was besotted with the baby too. It was the closest I had come to having a real brother myself and I spent every spare moment I could with David. Mum was around there all the time, however. It transformed her beyond all recognition into a loving, warm-hearted mother.

Now I understand she saw this as her second chance, a God-given opportunity to put things right between her and her son. As a ten-year-old, however, I perceived none of these things. I remember lying in bed that night thinking to myself: 'There isn't much love here for me as it is, am I going to have to share that now?'

Chapter 5

Love Me, Love My Dog

One bright summer's day when I was fourteen, I was driving through the suburbs of west London in the cab of my father's lorry. This was something I often did during the school holidays. I enjoyed being out and about with him, getting to see different parts of London and the surrounding countryside. At that time he was working on the new runway at Heathrow Airport, so there was an extra excitement to the trips we made. We were driving through the town of West Drayton in Middlesex when, without any warning, he suddenly pulled off the road and into the drive of a house. There was a small sign hanging from the porch. It read: 'Mrs Stephens' Boarding Kennels'.

At first I just sat there, unsure what was going on.

'Come on, are you getting out or not?' my father said, swinging open the driver's door.

'Why?'

'You wanted a dog, didn't you?'

I thought my heart was going to jump out of my mouth.

As I'd entered my teens, I had increasingly found the affection I needed in dogs and the pets we had at home –

44

even if they brought as much heartache as comfort at times.

By now we had moved out of the Clyde Flats on Rylston Road into an upstairs flat in a property on Rowallan Road. It was bigger than the old place, but still cramped. There was only one bedroom; the front room doubled up as a bedsit for me. We had a sitting room and a scullery.

Bluey came with us but soon after we moved he became ill. The talkative charmer of the past disappeared and he became a quieter, sadder creature. He developed the habit of picking at his coat, which left him looking in a terrible state. It was soon clear that his days were numbered, but the end – when it came – was still poignant.

Bluey had been sitting on the bottom of his cage for three days, becoming quieter and quieter. Then one day he got up and seemed chirpier. We let him out of the cage and he was his old affectionate self. He climbed up my dad's arm and sort of nibbled at it as if he was kissing him. Then he hopped around, performing the same routine with each of us. Thinking he was better, we put him back in his cage. He died that night. He had obviously wanted to say goodbye. I was mortified.

By then my father in particular had realized I wouldn't be settled without a pet of some kind. I really did love the companionship. That same week he suddenly appeared with a black and white old English rabbit I called Domino.

But my run of bad luck hadn't ended. Domino soon became sick. One day I was carrying him to the vet, covered in a blue blanket. I can still remember the blanket, it had white swallows on it. Suddenly he screamed. I had never heard a rabbit scream before and before I knew it he had died in my arms. It broke my heart. I was nowhere near the surgery and was just as far away from home so I ended up running to the nearest house I knew, that of my mother's in-laws the Cowpers. Nora Cowper was related through marriage to my mother's brother Sonny and lived off Lillie Road with her three daughters, Jacquie, Geraldine and Debbie. They were a lovely family who meant a lot to me. The moment Nora opened the door I burst into tears. She took me under her wing and dealt with poor Domino. 'Give her to me Janice, I'll lay her to rest here,' she said. With the girls we went to the garden where we conducted a little burial service before placing her in a box in a hole in the corner.

We never found out what had killed Domino so suddenly. The poor thing may have caught an infection, but we simply didn't know.

For a time, I can remember feeling I was a curse to these animals. As I scampered after my father towards the doors of Mrs Stephens' Boarding Kennels, however, all that was forgotten.

We rang the bell and a woman appeared. It was clearly the owner, Mrs Stephens.

She was expecting us. 'Mr Fennell, hello. Would you like to come with me and I'll show you the puppies,' she smiled.

There were all manner of dogs in the kennels at the rear of the house. But Mrs Stephens made a beeline for a pen where I saw three black and white Border collie puppies leaping around in a cage.

I'd fantasized about having my own dog for years, of course. Usually I imagined myself having a Lassie dog, a collie. Now all I wanted was a Border collie – one of these Border collies.

'Two of them are four guineas, one of them is five,' Mrs Stephens said, brisk and businesslike.

My dad asked me to choose. I knew already which one I wanted. One of the trio had a lovely tricoloured little face – black with white and little bits of tan. From the moment I'd walked up to the kennel he hadn't stopped staring at me.

'That one please, Dad,' I said.

'That's the five-guinea one,' Mrs Stephens replied.

'Oooh, she's got expensive tastes like her mother,' he smiled.

He was a beautiful dog. Mrs Stephens picked him up and offered him to my father.

'It's Janice's,' he said gently, counting out the money. 'Give it to her.'

He was about eight or nine weeks old. Mrs Stephens told me to put him on the floor to see how he moved; his little legs wobbled and his tail was wagging. I wanted to pick him up and love him. I couldn't believe he was mine.

We got back into the lorry and drove home. I was nervous as well as excited. The poor little puppy was traumatized at having been separated from his litter. No matter how much I cuddled him he cried all the way home. Dad understood this better than I did. 'He's frightened. He's got to learn to trust us,' he said.

When we got him home he ran around the flat like a dervish then peed on the floor. My dad and I looked at each other with horror. We were both thinking the same thing. Mum.

'Perhaps we should have put him out in the garden,' I said as I went to get the cleaning materials.

For once, however, Mum confounded us.

When she came home from work that evening she didn't worry about the fading patch of damp on the carpet. Instead she seemed genuinely interested in the new arrival. 'Hello, you're nice,' she said to the puppy.

Her interest didn't extend to being affectionate to the dog, however. He started climbing up and she stepped back. 'Don't jump up at me, dear,' she told him firmly. She then ignored him for the rest of the evening.

Shane, as I had soon christened him, brought me and my father closer than we'd been for a long time. Dad loved him too and training him became our joint project.

Dad sorted out his vaccinations. Then we did obedience training in the traditional way. He was very concerned that we should be responsible about it all. 'We want him to be a well-trained dog, a happy dog,' he would say to me. And in that respect, we succeeded brilliantly.

Soon we had taught him to walk to heel and to come. And soon both Dad and I were taking him out for walks around the neighbourhood. Dad also used to take him out in the lorry during the daytime. He became a member of the family in a way no other pet had, apart from Bluey.

Mum treated him like another child. She wasn't nasty to him; she thought he was cute, although she never warmed to him. She fed him and let him out into the back garden. But her main concern was that he always wiped his feet and didn't get things dirty and kept the house clean. We had to groom him too so that there were no hairs anywhere.

In effect she behaved towards Shane as she had towards me – to such an extent that she wouldn't let him go out on the street with the other dogs from the neighbourhood.

Mum disapproved of me mixing with the rest of the kids from the street. If I was sitting out on the coping she would appear at the top of the stairs: 'Janice, come in here, don't do that, that's what common people do.' She was a snob. She couldn't see that we were 'common' too.

Shane was soon being treated the same way. She said once she didn't want him being a street urchin. She didn't want him mixing with a lower class of dog!

Mum was too wrapped up in her own life to keep a constant eye on us, however. And soon Shane was very much integrated with the other dogs on the street.

The leader of the local 'pack' was Bobby, an old mongrel, a foxy type of dog with pointed ears. Bobby was the street's guard dog. When Shane first arrived as a puppy, Bobby was very protective of him whenever I took him out. We used to giggle because if any other dogs came near Bobby would adopt a stance, growling and staring aggressively. He was fourteen years old, slow and frail looking. But it was a convincing act nevertheless.

As Shane grew, however, old Bobby was relieved of the duty. The passing of the torch came one day when Shane was about nine months old and a big black dog appeared around the corner. Bobby growled at him as usual but it had no effect. For a moment it looked as if there was going to be trouble, but it was Shane who drove him away. Afterwards Bobby licked Shane's face, as if thanking him for what he'd done. From then on Bobby and Shane became a duo.

Like Digger, Shane opened doors for me. In many ways he allowed me to become a part of the community for the first time. I became friendly with the children who owned Bobby and another dog, Lucky. We'd all jump on a bus up to Putney Heath together where we'd let the dogs run free at the weekends.

My mother disapproved of this, of course, but less because of the friends I was making than because of the mess Shane used to come back in. I recall one Sunday lunchtime when we went to Putney Heath but got caught out by a wet mist that came down. The ground became very heavy and the dogs got clatted up. We were lucky to be allowed back on the bus to Fulham.

The dogs were sweating heavily, too, and the smell they gave off was terrible. We went upstairs, giggling whenever a passenger clambered up the steps only to return to the lower deck when they were hit by the stench.

As we drew closer to home, however, the laughter faded. My mother was having friends around for tea. I thought to myself: 'She's going to kill me.'

I tried to sneak Shane in so that I could give him a bath straight away. My mother wasn't there but my father was. He loved Shane and helped me get him in the bath. We were having great fun and games cleaning him when my mother reappeared.

I remember she turned absolutely white with rage. The fact that Dad was laughing only made things worse.

The respect for animals I had inherited from my grandmother and Great-Uncle Jim deepened as I grew older. But it also brought me into conflict with other members of the family who had a different outlook.

At first my sensitivity to the feelings of other living creatures showed itself in small ways. My dad liked cowboys and he used to take me to see westerns. I would get upset when the horses were brought down. I didn't know it at the time, but they were using potholes or tripwires. To me there was nothing clever about killing animals. My nan and my Great-Uncle Jim had taught me to respect and care for horses and such activities went against this principle.

And by an early age I had begun to rebel against the idea of eating animals. I can vividly remember that when my mother used to take me to Manzi's eel and pie shop, I would watch the wriggling eels and think, 'There is no way on earth I am going to eat them.' But when I voiced my feelings she didn't like it.

On one occasion at the butcher's my mother asked for veal. I asked what it was and was so horrified when they explained how it was produced that I blurted out the words, 'I'm not eating that.'

'You'll eat it and like it, my girl,' my mother snapped.

'Sounds like you've got a revolution on your hands,' the butcher smiled as she dragged me out of the shop.

That night at home I sat at the table, the veal on my plate in front of me, locked in a war of wills with my parents. I knew if I put it into my mouth I would be sick. I was eleven. It seemed so cruel.

I paid the price for that one. My father didn't stop chastising me for days afterwards for having upset my mother. It was a small victory, however. Elsewhere I was powerless to impose my feelings about animal cruelty – especially when it came to dogs.

The way some members of the family treated their dogs appalled me. My mother's brother Uncle George had a dog called Bruce, a white German shepherd they had got from Battersea Dogs' Home. I remember George used to lay out small penny bars of chocolate on the kitchen table in their wrapping and tell Bruce not to touch them. He used to think it was marvellous that he could come back half an hour later and find the chocolate still intact. Bruce would sit there looking at the chocolate and drooling, with the saliva dripping down his mouth. I thought this was wicked, it was torment. I used to cry when they put the chocolate on the table.

All the family used to say, 'Oh don't be so stupid, the dog's got to know what's what.' They would have a go at me for feeling like this. But my stomach hurt. I would sit in the chair and curl up and say nothing. I felt like running away, but I also felt I couldn't leave the dog because I would be abandoning him. I knew what it was like to be left alone with pain, to suffer on your own.

The more I learned about dogs, the more convinced I became of their intelligence and sensitivity. And the more determined I became to spare them such treatment.

No dog did more to convince me of its smartness than Shane. That dog was so clever he could tell the difference between the noise my father's lorry made when it was full and when it was empty. Dad often used to take Shane out in his cab if he had a full load and a delivery to make. If Shane detected an empty lorry he would lie quietly. If he sensed there was a day out in it for him, he would get very excited.

He also had an amazing sense of direction. One night he went missing. My father had said that he was going to take him for a walk but had been distracted. Suddenly we realized Shane wasn't there. We panicked. Then Dad said: 'Hold on a minute.' He went out, following their regular walk to the local Labour Exchange. There lay Shane. A woman came out and said he'd been lying there for an hour. That was his walk. He was so well trained we never bothered putting him on a lead, so he had gone there and waited.

For the next few years, Shane and I became utterly inseparable. It was literally a case of love me, love my dog. I went absolutely everywhere with him. Everyone knew that if they invited me to a party then Shane would come with me. I used to go to a youth club and I would take him there with me. I was the only one who did this, yet the amazing thing was that nobody ever questioned it. All the teenagers loved him and he loved all the attention. We were a couple, he was my best mate. If people thought it was odd, I didn't care. Shane had shown more loyalty and affection to me than any other creature I'd come across. And by now he'd proven that he would defend me to the death if necessary.

The first time I saw Shane in full flight was one Saturday afternoon.

We lived within a short walk of Craven Cottage, home to the then mighty Fulham Football Club. Every fortnight Fulham would be playing at home and all the roads around the ground would become crowded with traffic. Visiting fans used to park down our street, so if my dad was away, it was me and my mum's job to protect the parking space outside our house.

It wasn't a particularly scientific process. We'd just set two chairs down and then put brooms across them. On this particular day, sometime during the early 1960s, my mother was putting the chairs out. I was upstairs playing The Beatles. I had a little grey portable record player. One of my uncles worked at EMI so I used to get records early. Suddenly I was aware that Shane was going ballistic through the window next to me. When I leaned out I soon saw why.

Some men had pulled up in a car and one was trying to remove the chairs. My mum was hanging on to them and one guy was trying to separate her from them. There was a real commotion. The men were using unpleasant language and my mother was shouting for help so I ran downstairs. As I went through the door, I sensed that Shane would be behind me and that I should keep him in the house. So I shut both the front door and the gate behind me. But I had underestimated him.

Suddenly Shane appeared out of nowhere. He cleared the gate in one bound, launching himself from the step. Somehow I grabbed him, put my arms around his chest and held on to him for dear life. He was fit to kill. But I sensed these guys weren't nice people and might hurt him badly.

Shane's arrival had the desired effect, however. They jumped into the car and drove off in a hurry. The wheels were spinning, leaving tyre tracks. As the car disappeared down the road, neighbours came running out. Mum was in a state, Shane was panting like crazy in my arms. Everyone was full of praise for Shane. What a great dog he was, and how loyal. 'No one's going to hurt you or your mum while he's around,' they said.

I was on my own with Shane when he underlined how true that was.

Ron and the family had moved near Olympia and I had popped over to see them one Saturday afternoon. Shane and I stayed there until early evening and set off home at about 7 p.m. It was a measure of how safe the streets of London were in those days that there was nothing unusual in this. I thought nothing of walking three miles across a busy part of the city unattended. No one would allow a young girl to do that now. We were walking down a short cut off the North End Road when we passed two lads sitting on a wall. They started whistling at me as lads do. 'All right, darling.'

As usual Shane was quite a way ahead of me. That was the way it was. He knew the way home. I did what I knew I should do, which was ignore them, keep my head down and just keep going.

Unfortunately these two weren't so easily shaken off and they started following me.

'What's a matter with you then, sweetheart?' said one.

'Don't run away, darling,' the other shouted when I started to walk faster.

I was just beginning to panic, sure that something unpleasant was going to happen, when Shane appeared from nowhere, snarling. He went straight at the two lads, who just turned and fled the other way, one of them with Shane hanging on to his bottom. I called him back and we ran all the way home.

Later on that weekend, funnily enough, I went to see my nephew in Fulham again. I looked down at Shane playing with the kids, the boys dive-bombing at him. He was rolling around on the floor letting them do whatever they wanted.

This was the wonderful, kind, dopey dog that would let children do anything, that would play with squirrels. But in a moment he could be transformed. To us and the family he was the perfect dog. He was obedient, he was full of playfulness. Yet he would have protected us to the death.

Like most people I thought a dog was part of the family and therefore under the family's protection. It would be many years before I realized how misconceived an idea that was.

Chapter 6

Departures

By the time I was in my mid-teens other members of the family had sensed the problems that existed between me and my parents.

The loneliness I felt at home was hard to bear at times. Sometimes I would feel physically sick. I regularly cried myself to sleep. I felt a sense of abandonment. Often I felt there was no hope. My unhappiness was all too obvious when we visited relatives. I did my best to appear the dutiful, polite and pleasant young woman, but it didn't convince many people.

Things came to a head one Christmas with my cousin Doreen. We had begun spending Christmases with her and her husband Reg at their home in Welwyn Garden City. Doreen had always been the kindest of all my relatives. She'd seen the way my mother treated me and had decided it was time to raise the subject of adopting me. But it was only years later that I heard the story of what happened that day.

The air must have been bristling with electricity. 'You obviously don't love her,' Doreen had said to my mother when the two of them were alone, clearing up after the Christmas turkey. 'You don't know what I feel for her,' my mother had apparently snapped back. 'Besides, you've got a daughter of your own to look after you.'

If anything explained the complex way in which my mother regarded me, that exchange did. Her feelings for me were strong, of that I have no doubt. She did love me, even if it was in a cold and unemotional way. I also have no doubt that she felt she was making a perfectly good job of raising me. Why wouldn't she? She was doing what she believed was the right thing. Her words that day confirmed something fundamental, however. At the root her feelings were more selfish. To her my most important role – for now, at least – was to be there for her, to give her the support she felt I was put on this earth to provide. No one was going to deny her that.

The matter was never raised again. Apparently my father had come into the room while the argument was going on. When Doreen repeated her offer he was incredulous – and very angry. 'I can't believe you of all people would say that,' he told Doreen.

Needless to say, we saw less of them after that.

Inevitably, as I got older, matters came to a head occasionally. I remember one day my mother and I were in the bathroom squabbling. I had told her I didn't think something was fair. And that had lit the blue touch paper.

'Don't ever tell me what's right and wrong,' she'd said.

'Aren't I entitled to an opinion?' I'd said.

'No.'

'But that's not fair.'

The next thing I knew she had whacked me hard across the head.

'That's what fair is,' she said. 'Life isn't fair.'

The irony was that I walked down to the florist and spent all my pocket money on flowers for her. I knew my father would take it out on me if my mother stayed upset. So I did what was necessary to keep the peace.

Eventually, however, I snapped. I was about sixteen and Dad and I had had an argument about something. He wouldn't let me put my side, insisting: 'This is the way it is in my house.' I was so upset.

There was no getting through to them. I couldn't see a light at the end of the tunnel. So that night I waited for the house to go dark, and I picked up my teddy, quietly put Shane on his lead and slipped out of the house. London was shrouded in darkness. It was a cold, drizzly night and the streets were empty. I was wearing jeans, a t-shirt and a heavy brown cardigan, which was getting heavier with each step from the drizzle. For a while I didn't know where I was going. I just walked towards Fulham Palace Road, Shane by my side, clutching my teddy tight. By the time I reached there the idea had formed in my head that I was going to see David, the one person in the world I really loved at that particular moment.

I crossed the Thames at Putney Bridge, continuing along the edge of Wimbledon Common and down into Wimbledon where Ron and Anne were now living. I remember I arrived at their doorstep, sopping wet, at four in the morning. I had walked something like five miles.

Ron was just getting up. He was working with my dad

at Blue Circle, the cement company near Wandsworth Bridge. As it happened my dad was also on an early that day. Ron told him I was at his house and he jumped straight into his lorry to collect me.

The drive back from south London was one of the worst journeys I've ever made. My father and I sat there in silence, my mind filled with thoughts of what my mother would do to me when I got back. 'I'm in for it now,' I told myself.

But when we got home, we discovered the house still dark.

My father bundled me in, telling me to keep quiet. 'Thank God for that,' he said. 'Your mother's not awake yet.' It was still 7 or 8 a.m. He just said: 'Don't you ever tell her,' before leaving me and going back to work.

When Mum got up I pretended that nothing had happened. She never knew I had run away.

It would have upset her. And, of course, she mustn't be upset at any cost.

It had been clear early on that my schooling was intended to prepare me for a job. I was a girl, after all. What else did I think I was going to do?

Apart from conspiring to separate me from my cousin Les, my parents had taken next to no interest in my education. I recall one year my school report was so bad I ripped up the report book and discarded it in a dustbin on the way home. It would never have occurred to my parents to ask whether I had received a report.

When I went back to school and was eventually asked

where the book was, I just said: 'My mum's still got it.' The school wasn't much more interested in my education than my parents, truth be told. The fact that the report book had failed to materialize was quickly forgotten. I can't even remember getting another report.

The only time my parents intervened was to prevent me from doing the things I had set my heart on. I wanted to do art, for instance. But they wouldn't let me. I had to do cookery, 'because that will be more use'.

So it was little surprise that when I left school, I wasn't fit for much.

My first job was at the Post Office Savings Bank. I didn't like it so I applied for a job at Barber's on North End Road between Fulham Broadway and Lillie Road. It was very much like *Are You Being Served*. I worked on scarves and handkerchiefs.

One evening I came home from work to find my father there, a sheepish look on his face.

He soon spat out what was on his mind.

'We've found a new flat,' he said. 'Your mother likes it.'

I had known Mum didn't like the people in the flat beneath us; she thought they were common. For Mum to moan about where she lived was nothing unusual so I didn't take much notice.

'Fine,' I said. To be honest, I was more interested in taking Shane out for his evening walk. By then Shane was all that mattered to me. I certainly didn't care about a new flat.

Then Dad delivered the bombshell.

'We won't be able to take Shane,' he said, staring at the

floor as he spoke. I looked at my dad in disbelief. He couldn't look me in the eye.

Moments later my mother arrived back from work. She, of course, expected me to be delighted. She took umbrage when I suggested I wouldn't go without Shane.

'We can't take him there,' she said. 'And we need a bigger place, because you need your own bedroom.'

I was too traumatized to speak. 'I don't want to talk about it,' I said before heading off to bed. I didn't sleep a wink that night. I was in a state of shock.

I went to work as normal the next day and when I got home that night, Shane had gone. Dad had given him to the Blue Cross, a rescue centre nearby. After four years he had gone in twenty-four hours.

I wasn't the only one who was devastated. As Mum was walking around that night rabbiting on about how exciting it was going to be getting new curtains, my dad and I kept looking at each other. That night I heard Dad in the bedroom sobbing.

I didn't sleep, of course. I just lay there, thinking that I couldn't believe they'd done it to me. I couldn't take it in.

A few days later we moved house and I got my nice new room. Big deal. The worst thing was that some of the family were so dismissive about it. 'Oh, it's only a bloody dog,' someone said.

Others, like Doreen, couldn't mention it. By now she had lost Tinker, one of my early companions, and knew what it was like to be parted from a beloved pet. And she knew how important Shane had been to me.

For me it was the last straw. We'd only been at the new

place a few days when I caught a bus across London to Holborn and the main recruitment centre for the Women's Royal Naval Service, the Wrens. I'd made my mind up soon after Shane was taken away from me. I'd checked out the procedure and found that it required me to submit an application then undergo a morning's test. I turned up early for the 10 a.m. interview. I marched in there saying to myself: 'I'm going to do this.' The process consisted of three sets of interviews and various aptitude tests. I had to have an eye test and a medical as well. I acquitted myself pretty well, I thought. I found out later that of the thirty girls who were there for an interview that morning only two would get in. It would be a few weeks before I discovered whether I was one of them.

I headed home that evening and told my parents. Dad had been in the Army, my mother's son had been in the RAF, so I thought at least my father would be pleased. His reaction was, as ever, coloured by my mother. So I got two hours of silence.

Over the coming days and weeks, the atmosphere remained frosty. I overheard Mum in the kitchen saying, 'They're very fussy, she probably won't get in.'

In time, however, this changed. The next time I overheard her she was talking about the letter that must be due any day now. My mum worked at the Ministry of Defence, so she probably knew what she was talking about. 'If she's got in it will be a big envelope, if she hasn't it will be just a letter,' I heard her saying to my father.

A few days later she came up the stairs carrying a big brown manila envelope. She thrust it into my hand, then stormed away. She wouldn't talk to me for days afterwards.

I'd love to say I joined up out of a sense of duty, of obligation to Queen and Country, but I would be lying. As I looked at the papers I simply thought: 'At last, this is my ticket out of here.'

Chapter 7

Calls of Duty

As the train rolled out of Paddington Station and steamed through the outskirts of London into the open countryside I felt a confusing mixture of emotions. I was on my way to HMS *Dauntless*, the Wrens' training camp in Reading. A part of me was quietly exhilarated. I had celebrated my eighteenth birthday that spring, but it was only now that I really felt I was beginning to come of age. It was as if I had been let loose on the wider world. But at the same time another part of me was filled with a fear of the unknown, an insecurity about whether I'd be up to the challenge ahead of me.

At least I soon realized I wasn't alone in my feelings. At Reading I was met by a big blue troop-carrying lorry with the letters 'RN' for Royal Navy on the cabin door. It was crammed with girls from as far afield as the Hebrides, Wales and Cornwall. We all climbed on board, then sat there clinging to our single suitcases as we bumped along the roads. On the drive to the camp the atmosphere was friendly but apprehensive. There wasn't much eye contact, but when there was I recognized the same blend of excitement and trepidation that I was feeling. As we passed through the base's checkpoint, I'm sure most of us saw it as HMS *Daunting* rather than *Dauntless*.

HMS *Dauntless* was where you learned to salute, march and behave with the discipline expected of a member of Her Majesty's Armed Forces. The first few hours were a whirl of activity. To begin with we were issued with our temporary uniform, our 'blues'. High fashion they were not. They were basically overalls made of canvas, something you'd never have seen near Barber's in Fulham in a million years unless you were looking at the road-sweepers on the North End Road outside.

Then we were shown to our accommodation block where we were allocated a 'cabin', a small cubicle with a single bunk bed. There were something like a dozen of these in each block, so that in all there were twenty-four girls under the one roof. I shared a cabin with a Scots girl, Ingrid. Being so far away from her family, she was suffering terribly from the one emotion I didn't feel – homesickness. I took the top bunk. In the darkness that first night the air inside and outside our cabin was filled with the sound of muffled sobbing. It seemed to ripple down the corridor. By the time it reached us Ingrid was crying so hard and uncontrollably the metallic bunk was shaking. I didn't know what to say or do. So I joined in. I think we all cried that night.

In some respects, the tough upbringing my parents had given me proved a good preparation for life in the services. From the moment we walked out on to the parade ground that first week, discipline was everything, but that was fine with me. You knew where you stood, the rules were the rules. And, unlike at home, there were no mixed messages. It was simple. As long as you did your job you were OK. I really enjoyed it.

I never quite got used to the 6 a.m. roll call at the parade ground. But marching, for some reason, was something that came naturally to me. I relished it, and found myself being made a 'marker', the lead-off Wren in our division.

The feeling that the world was opening up to me at last was tangible in the Wrens. As I listened to the experiences of the longer-serving officers, I heard them talking about their time on overseas posting. Raw recruits like me would naturally talk about their ambitions. Some people fancied the Far East, others talked of going to Africa. I'd become rather taken with the idea of Malta, where there was a small contingent of Wrens at the time. Back then few people went on Mediterranean holidays. It sounded rather exotic and exciting, and I set my sights on getting there one day.

Unfortunately there were familiar forces conspiring against me. From the outset, I knew my mother was determined to make my stay in the Wrens as short as possible.

The Wrens differed from almost every other part of the armed forces in that you didn't officially 'sign up' for them. You had two weeks in which to decide whether you wanted to stay or not. If you did, you then committed yourself to four years.

At the end of the first week in Reading we were given a weekend off. The only condition, however, was that we spent each night within HMS *Dauntless*. On the Saturday morning I decided I'd better visit Mum and Dad. They'd been on the phone all week, apparently. The petty officer had come up to me at one point and said: 'Your parents ring a lot, don't they?'

I can still recall the fuss they made over me that Saturday. I'd never been treated so nicely. Of course they spent the day trying to persuade me to come back home at the end of my initial fortnight. 'You don't have to stay,' they kept saying. 'Your mum really misses you.' They even drove me back to Reading that evening. In my cabin that night I felt a huge sense of guilt. 'How can I do this to her?' I thought to myself. But, for the first time in my life, I actually felt I belonged somewhere. When the fortnight came to an end I decided to stay on and make a go of it in the Wrens.

I completed six weeks at *Dauntless* before being transferred to the naval barracks at Chatham, in Kent, where I would get a further eight weeks' training for a specific job, in my case working in the stores. We had by now progressed to the full Wrens uniform. Again it wasn't the sort of thing any fashion-conscious girl would be seen dead wearing back in London, especially with Carnaby Street in the grip of mini-skirt fever: a white shirt, black tie and jacket with a black skirt so long you could barely see an ankle, let alone a knee or a flash of thigh. I remember as a joke telling one of the older petty officers that it felt as if we were wearing clothes from the war. A thin smile crept across her face. 'They *are* from the war,' she said. I didn't believe it until I checked the tag. Sure enough there was a mark saying '1944'. We were wearing clothes that were more than twenty years old. Some of the girls hated it, but I on the other hand thought it was the bee's knees, particularly when I donned the white so-called 'flight deck' hat. It looked so smart and brought you respect. I felt a million dollars whenever I went out in full uniform.

My mother's attempts to blackmail me into coming back home continued, of course. But from then on I started lying to her. When she phoned to ask if I was coming home at the weekend I'd say: 'Sorry, I'm on duty.' So much for my notions of having grown up. I didn't know how to say no without upsetting her.

The truth of the matter was that I was having the time of my life.

Life on the camp was fun. I socialized like I had never done before in my life. There were dances and people like Lulu and Brian Poole & The Tremeloes played.

I knew it was a transient kind of life. You didn't make permanent friends because you knew you were moving on. So boyfriends were a complication none of us needed. We'd go out in groups of a dozen of us and just have a good time.

In truth I wasn't the most natural sailor in the world, I have to admit. I remember the kerfuffle I caused when I was first fitted with a respirator. The overwhelming rubbery smell of the gas mask was too much for me and I backed away from the petty officer who had drawn the short straw of fitting it on me. When they did put it on, I went woozy. 'We've got a fainter here!' I remember the petty officer shouting. I never quite got used to the regular gas mask drills. I even gave my mask a name, Cecil, in the hope I would come to see it as a friend, but to no avail. The masks had to be tested on a regular basis in a gas chamber where a tear gas canister had been released. On one occasion I ripped my mask off in the chamber. The reaction I got was terrible. It was a dreadful experience and only added to my horror of the regular drills. In the end friends volunteered to test the mask for me. I never really overcame my fear.

My reputation as a 'fainter' stuck with me as my training went on. It was cemented by another incident on the parade ground one morning. At Reading we'd marched to taped music, at Chatham we marched to a magnificent Marine band. One morning I'd gone out with a heavy cold. I had my greatcoat on, a big, heavy, warm thing. Underneath it I was sweating and shivering. At some point my head began spinning. I knew full well by now that the secret of being able to stand still for long periods of time was to fix your eyes on a spot. But that was impossible as my head spun more and more. I felt myself teetering. Fortunately the petty officer alongside me had spotted me. I remember him shouting out the order for 'Two gentlemen to assist, quick march.' Two Marines arrived just as I keeled over. They caught me and carried me back to my billet. I was never allowed to forget that.

My feelings for animals also became something of a running joke. Learning to shoot was not compulsory within the Wrens but it was something I was keen to try. My teacher was a male chief petty officer who clearly hadn't come across anyone with my sensibilities.

At the camp's shooting range I had to lie down on my belly and take aim at the assorted targets. We were a good thirty yards away. But as I lined up my rifle I saw the targets were in the form of animals. I think there was a deer, a lion and a bird of some kind. My first attempt was woeful so I asked whether I could try the alternative targets, the simple round, bull's-eye kind.

The chief petty officer laughed to himself, but when I tried again with these targets I fared much better. From then on, whenever I turned up for practice he'd rib me about it. 'Here she comes, get out the round targets,' he'd smile.

Despite all this I completed my basic training at Chatham around November 1966. We had a passing-out ceremony to mark the occasion.

The barracks were open for inspection by the public that day. As we prepared for the main march past, I remember rushing around making sure everything was 'ship shape and Bristol fashion'. I couldn't have imagined it just months earlier. My distaste for housework had always been intense but here I was on my knees cleaning dust until the last second.

The passing-out parade was one of the showpiece events of the year at Chatham. All the 'scrambled egg' top brass were there. We marched past, doing a well-drilled eyes right as we filed by our commanding officer. I felt a sense of pride at what I'd achieved. I hoped it was something my parents would share too, but I was soon brought back down to earth.

I approached my father, quietly brimming with anticipation that I might get some of the praise from him that I'd always yearned for. 'Guess what your mum said?' he smiled, as ever making this moment about her rather than me. 'There's our girl. She's the only one with dirty knees.'

In my haste to get out of the barracks on to the parade ground in time I'd forgotten to clean the last remnants of dust off my black tights. No one else on the parade ground had seen fit to even refer to it. Trust my mother to make something of it.

To be honest, I expected no better. I just laughed and said: 'Thanks, Mum.' It only made me more determined to get as far as possible away from home.

My wish was soon granted. My first posting was to Arbroath in Scotland. I didn't know there was anywhere as cold as that on earth. I couldn't get enough layers of clothes on to stay warm. I remember I spent my nineteenth birthday there the following March. The base's fire crew took me out for the night, I seem to remember. They bought me a lovely gold bracelet as a present, which I really treasured. Part of me, though, spent the night wishing they'd get a call-out so I could find somewhere to warm up.

It was when I came home for my first extended leave from Scotland that my family really turned the screw to get me out of the Wrens.

My mother had always taken tranquillizers. 'Tablets for her nerves,' was how my father always referred to them.

Addiction was not a word that was part of the everyday vocabulary then. But I think it would have fitted well enough. When I came back for a brief stay in London she seemed disoriented, subdued, at other times irritable. My father confirmed that she'd been taking more than her normal dosage. He told me she couldn't cope with me being all those miles away.

Even then I sensed what was really going on. Her looks had started to go and she wasn't a glamorous woman any more. She would say to me: 'You will take care of me, won't you?' She was terrified of being alone. She was petrified of being put in a home, even though she was only in her late forties. By playing on my guilt about leaving her she was acting in her own interest again. She knew that if I stayed close I would be able to look after her.

For a while I had kidded myself that I had made a clean break from the family. But that was far from the truth. On the long train journey back up to Scotland I realized my duty lay with them rather than the Wrens. I was so unsettled by the state my mother had been in that weekend that when I got back to the ship I went to see my commanding officer. I asked for a posting nearer home and cited compassionate grounds.

'You do realize this is going to prejudice your chances of an overseas posting, don't you?' she told me.

There is nothing so awful as seeing your dreams die before your very eyes, but that's what I saw that day. From the tone of the officer's voice and the disapproving look on her face it was clear that was the end of that particular fantasy.

So instead of the Mediterranean I went to HMS *Heron*, in Yeovilton, Somerset.

Somerset was beautiful. I was really happy there. But the pressure to come home remained great. Each time I went I was treated to the latest instalment of the sob story. 'She needs you here.' 'You don't know what your being so far away is doing to your mother's nerves.' In the end I relented.

It sounds weak now, but I couldn't rid myself of the feelings of guilt. I felt that it was my fault that my mother was not well. I was somehow letting her down because I wasn't fitting into the world as she saw it. After all, since starting school there had been only one road down which I was supposed to travel. I was supposed to be married with children by now. Instead I'd done this strange, unnatural thing and gone off to the Wrens. The fact that I hadn't really found myself within the Wrens had laid the doubts. My mother had exploited them to the full.

I asked for an early discharge on compassionate grounds. I left the Wrens in October 1968. I'd been in there just over two years, half the time I'd expected to serve. I was back on Civvy Street again.

I arrived back in London, a young woman of twenty but still without the first clue about what I wanted to do with my life. At first I went to work at the Blue Circle cement plant at the Thameside wharf near Wandsworth Bridge where my father was still employed as a lorry driver. I worked in the office but didn't think much of that, so I headed off to central London to a job agency.

How different the job market was then! When I went to the agency I was given eight jobs to interview for. Each interview went well and by the end of the day I was having to apologize to my prospective employers, telling them I'd get back to them. 'I'll let you know if I want the job tomorrow.' I had no qualifications apart from a City & Guilds '150' certificate in catering and the call of the kitchen didn't appeal to me. But I could answer the phone, was a quick learner and fell into a job as a receptionist in an advertising agency in South Street, off South Audley Street.

The family were on at me about getting married and settling down. To be honest, I hadn't even considered it as a possibility. I hadn't been at the agency long when all that changed.

Tony Knight was part of the production team. He was a very handsome, smart, clever guy with a wicked sense of humour. He made me laugh a lot, I enjoyed his company and he opened new worlds to me, such as going to the theatre and eating at restaurants. I remember he took me for an Indian meal on our first date. I hadn't fallen in love before, so when I did I fell hook, line and sinker. We started dating, going out to the pub and the cinema and theatre. I always remember the beaming smile he'd greet me with whenever we got together. It was all for me.

For obvious reasons we had to keep it quiet within the agency for a while. He'd slip surreptitious notes to me to arrange assignations. We'd make sure we steered clear of the watering holes that the rest of the agency used. It was fun. The secrecy of it all added to the allure, I think. When I was going out on a date with him I told my parents the old cliché about 'staying with a friend'.

By the spring of 1969, however, our secret was out in the open. The sparkling engagement ring on my finger was a bit of a giveaway.

It had begun as a semi-joke one Saturday night in the Prince of Wales, a pub in Wimbledon. Tony was a keen footballer and was having a conversation with a friend on the subject of his team, Fulham, and their arch-rivals in west London, Chelsea. To his friend's amazement I'd joined in the conversation. 'A woman who isn't bored by football! Will you marry me?' he'd quipped.

'Sorry, mate, she's already spoken for. I'm marrying her,' Tony had replied before turning to me. 'Aren't I?'

'Ask me again when you're sober,' I'd replied.

The next day, the phone went at home. It was Tony. 'I meant what I said last night. Will you marry me?' he said, a little less full of himself than the previous night, but sincere nonetheless.

I was lost for words. I slipped out of the flat that evening and met him in Wimbledon. By then I'd made my mind up to accept.

I suppose somewhere deep inside I harboured the feeling that this was the only way I was going to get away from my mother, that this was the one course of action she couldn't object to because it was the one that she had preordained for me from the outset. Marriage, children, a life of domesticity – that was what I was meant to do, so she couldn't argue against it now. At the time, however, such ideas were completely submerged. I was getting married for one reason and one reason only – the fact that I was hopelessly and utterly in love.

A few days after the proposal, Tony arrived at my home and asked to speak to my father alone in the living room. It was the day before my twenty-first birthday, I remember it vividly. Old-fashioned guy that he was, he wanted to ask my father's permission for his daughter's hand in marriage. I thought it was a lovely gesture but my father, typically, tried to make a joke of it.

'If you'd waited until tomorrow, you'd not have needed to ask,' he replied. My mother, naturally, couldn't resist having her say about my choice of husband. 'He's all right, but he wouldn't have been good looking enough for me,' was her comment when she first met Tony, if I remember correctly. No wonder I'd put off their meeting until the last possible moment.

We'd already planned a small twenty-first birthday party for the following night. It became a double celebration. I remember I had a new black and white, full-length dress. My hair was up. I really felt that I had come of age. It seemed like the happiest night of my life. Days later Tony took me to a fancy jeweller's up in Golders Green. I picked out a beautiful antique ring, a ruby in a Victorian crown setting with diamonds dotted around it. It cost £30, a lot of money in those days, certainly for Tony and me. It was the most beautiful object I had ever owned.

We got married at St Ethelreda's Church on Fulham Palace Road on 8 November 1969.

The details of that day have never dimmed in my memory. How could they? An hour or so before the service I seriously doubted I'd be going down the aisle at all. I had been to the hairdresser's and had begun getting ready at home. I was getting dressed along with my bridesmaids, the three Cowper girls, and another close friend, Diane Jones, who was my matron of honour.

Typically my mother had the best dress that day. My white gown had cost £36, her outfit almost £50. When I came to slip into the dress it looked like a false economy. I discovered that the zip was defective. No matter what I or anyone else did it kept giving out and breaking loose. There was only half an hour left before the service and I was getting into a real state. The Rolls-Royce my dad had got hold of for the day was sitting outside the house, ready to ferry the bridesmaids and Diane over to the church then come back to collect me and my father. But no one was going anywhere with my dress in disarray. Fortunately the Cowper girls had been accompanied by their ever-resourceful mother, Nora, who came to the rescue. She stepped in and said: 'Right, where's the needle and cotton?' before proceeding to stitch me into the dress. She did a fantastic job, particularly given the time available and the fact that I was a shaking, sobbing wreck.

No one knew the difference. In fact it might even have improved the look.

One of my cousins turned round to my mother when she saw me coming down the aisle. 'You don't outshine Jan today, Nona,' she apparently told her. The glare my mother gave her was designed to turn her to stone.

It was a lovely service and there was a joyous reception afterwards. Naturally all my family started singing and dancing. One thing I always recall was how content I felt. It was a very old-fashioned view of the world, I know. But I thought my life was fulfilled, as if I was somehow living up once more to my duties within the family. I thought this was what I was destined for. Everything was right in the world. When I walked down the aisle, I had no doubts that I was making a commitment for life. And I didn't ever think anything could go wrong.

Tony and I spent our wedding night at my parents' home. We had the place to ourselves. I'd kept my wedding dress on all through the night. Of course, by then I'd forgotten about the running repairs that Nora had performed earlier in the day. It was only as I started trying to get out of the dress that I remembered I was sewn into it. Tony quickly realized I was having a problem and offered to help.

'Is there anything I can do?' he asked sweetly.

I remember the look of shock on his face when I said: 'Well actually, yes, you can get a pair of scissors and cut me out of this.'

The first few years of marriage did nothing to dispel the rather romantic notions I had taken with me down the aisle. We moved to a house in Wimbledon. Then, in 1970, I became a mother. I was ecstatic when I gave birth to a baby boy, who – traditionalists that we were – we christened Anthony after his father.

By March 1972 we had our second child, a girl, Ellie.

Animals had faded into the background during those early years of marriage. In truth, I still thought that side of my life was doomed. I was sure that as soon as I got close to an animal it would be sure to disappear. I just said to myself, 'Stay away.'

Tony was an animal lover too, however. As we settled into family life, he persuaded me to have a ginger cat that we called Biscuit. Unbelievably, he was stolen. It only confirmed my view that as far as animals were concerned I was a curse.

In the summer of 1972, however, everything changed. Tony had been made redundant by the advertising agency when it lost the major account he worked on. In the past we had talked – half-jokingly – of moving to the countryside. Tony liked the idea of living away from the city, as I did. While we were considering what to do next, it suddenly became a serious possibility. Somehow, Lincolnshire became the focus of our attention. I had relatives living in the county and had often visited over the years. My Aunt Ciss lived near Lincoln, while another aunt had moved to the town of Wainfleet.

We put the house in Wimbledon on the market. In the meantime Tony headed for Lincolnshire to see what the property situation was up there. Before we knew it we'd sold our house in London and bought a house in a village inland from Skegness with the proceeds. It cost us just £3,500.

I can still remember the wave of excitement that washed over us when the dream of leaving London for the country-side became a reality. I had visions of the kids running around in huge open spaces, of the four of us living closer to nature and of a quieter, somehow calmer life than that we lived in London.

We had barely agreed to buy the new house when we decided that the final piece in the jigsaw would be a dog. In our minds, we both imagined yomping around the rolling countryside, our faithful companion at our side. Within days Tony turned up with a dog he had acquired from a local rescue centre. We christened her Purdey.

We didn't know what breed she was but we knew she was a pretty little thing and we liked her. She had a black body, with a white blaze on her face. Her legs were white with black specks, like a Dalmatian. By the time we had packed up our possessions to leave London, she was a fully integrated member of what I thought was the perfect family set-up. And now we were off to our perfect country home . . .

Chapter 8

The Edge of Nowhere

As the car crunched its way along the gravelly country lane and slowed down outside my new home, a sudden, terrible thought welled up in my mind. 'Oh God, what have we done?'

I was so wrapped up with the children, I had entrusted all the arrangements to Tony. Back in London, all I had known was that the house was in a village called Firsby about ten miles inland from the popular seaside resort of Skegness. I had been told it was a semi-detached, three-bedroom property with its own sizeable grounds, set on a quiet lane off the main road. I'm not sure what I had imagined it was going to look like. But no matter what I'd pictured in my head, it bore no resemblance to the rundown and ramshackle home I set eyes on that day in September 1972.

It looked as if it had been uninhabited for quite a while. Much of the paint was flaked and faded, the metal-framed windows were reddening with rust. The garden was huge, as I'd imagined it would be. But it was also wild and overgrown with shrubs and trees. I remember sitting in the car simply staring at it, wondering to myself how on earth we were going to survive here.

The neglected appearance of the place wasn't the only problem. In truth the house's defects were fixable, I knew that. It was the isolation that I couldn't get over.

There were six semi-detached houses on our lane, Eastfield Road, which was separate from the main village of Firsby, a mile or so down the road. I say main village, but it was hardly deserving of that word. It was minuscule.

If you sneezed as you were driving past you would miss it. There wasn't a shop there. The nearest post office, a mile away in a village called Great Steeping, also served as a shop, but it was barely that. The place had a stale, time-warped feel to it. The shelves were filled with tins and boxes that looked like they'd been there since the war. The walls were dotted with metallic signs for Oxo, Huntley & Palmer's biscuits and Brasso. I don't think I ever bought anything there.

I quickly discovered that the nearest general stores were in Spilsby, which was four miles away. That was also where the nearest doctor's surgery was and it had a weekly market. But even getting there was going to be a challenge. I didn't drive and buses were few and far between.

It was a huge culture shock. I was twenty-four. I had spent most of my life in London and all of a sudden here I was. In London buses came every few minutes, in Firsby they came twice a week. If we wanted anything in Wimbledon we had a shop across the street and within ten minutes I was on Wimbledon Broadway with its department stores and supermarkets, a cinema and a theatre. Now I had to put the children in the pram and walk four miles to reach a shop. My son Tony used to say that it wasn't the middle of nowhere, it was the edge of nowhere – without any shops. That just about summed it up.

The job of moving our belongings into the house dulled the disappointment for the rest of the day. The excitement of driving up from London allied to the first draughts of country air meant that Tony and the children slept like logs that night. I wish I could have joined them. As I lay in bed I tried to take in the enormity of what we'd done. I certainly didn't have any distractions as I lay there, my mind racing.

There were no streetlights so it was pitch black outside. It was unbelievably quiet. In London I'd been used to the faint, ever-present hum of the city. That night I lay thinking, 'Please, something, someone make a noise.'

I don't want to create the wrong impression here, I was happy about moving to the countryside. Nor am I criticizing my husband for his choice of house.

I hadn't been involved in choosing the place. I was so consumed by the children, particularly Ellie, the new baby, that I had left it to Tony. He had assured me that for £3,500 he had found a place that would suit us as a family and make financial sense as well. And he was probably right in that regard.

It was simply that amid all the excitement of moving out of London, I hadn't given the practicalities of what we were doing much thought. Until now. During that long, sleepless night I gave myself the talking-to that became a mantra over the coming months. I knew we had two young children, we had made the decision to come here and we had no choice but throw ourselves into it. I told myself: 'Look, there's no point in bringing London ways up here, this is the country, you get on with it.' So from the next morning onwards, that's what I did. I got on with it.

Looking back on it now, our naiveté makes me shake my head in quiet disbelief. We'd expected to up sticks and resume normal life without any problems in another part of the country. We were so convinced Tony would be able to get a job that we'd hardly considered it for a second. We'd made a little money on the sale of our London home so we thought we had a financial cushion to see us through the first few months. It didn't take long for us to be disavowed of both those ideas.

The cost of moving and setting ourselves up had, predictably, depleted the bank account. Tony quickly discovered that jobs were extremely thin on the ground. He'd hoped for something in sales or marketing, his areas of speciality. But within a week or so of arriving in Firsby he'd quickly realized there was little going. He'd already lowered his sights to more down-to-earth jobs, blue collar rather than white collar work. But even then there was little prospect of something cropping up.

At least there were plenty of ways of dealing with the frustration. During those early days Tony threw himself into tidying the place up. I still have an image of him lost in the wild expanse of the garden, thrashing his scythe through the overgrowth, like some explorer hacking his way through the Amazon jungle. The garden was two hundred feet long and overgrown, the grass so deep there were times when I'd look out through the kitchen window and struggle to spot Tony's head poking over the top.

Yet as we settled into life and got the house up and running, I began to see that there were plenty of positives to our new home. It wasn't Blenheim Palace. We had no central heating, only a tiny bathroom and three quite small bedrooms. But it was still an improvement on what we had had in London.

It was the first time in my life that I'd lived on two floors. Going out into the garden like that was something I'd never done before. I immediately had visions of clearing the garden and planting vegetables. I knew it was a distant dream but I pictured chickens running free at the bottom of the garden, goats providing us with milk; I imagined us becoming self-sufficient one day.

For the children, Tony in particular, it was a revelation, with all the space they could possibly want. What was more, before long, they had their grandparents around.

To me, becoming a mother was the greatest joy ever, not least because it completed the process of reconciliation I had slowly been undergoing with my own mother. Early on during my pregnancy I can remember that I kept telling myself I would not repeat the mistakes my mother had made. I would tell my children every day I loved them. I would let them be themselves rather than force them to abide by my ideas of what they should be. If I was ever unclear how to act, I should simply think of what my mother would have done then do the complete opposite.

Yet now I was a mother, I somehow understood her better. She had slowly begun to confide the truth about her first marriage. It had brought us closer. In truth I had begun to feel sorry for her. As the mother of a little baby boy, I empathized with the way she must have felt when she lost the custody battle over Ron. How would I have dealt with having Tony taken away from me? It didn't bear thinking about.

Sometimes my husband or close friends or relatives who knew her well would shake their heads when I said this. I was making excuses for her when her behaviour had been inexcusable, they said. To my mind, however, my mother was as much a victim as I was. Now that I had achieved this wonderful thing, this perfect family, how could I possibly punish her even more? Where was the harm in letting her share some of my happiness?

I'm not saying our relationship was transformed into something perfect in the wake of Tony's birth. Far from it. We still rubbed each other up the wrong way at every turn. Rows and long periods of non-communication were still the norm. Yet there was no question that our relationship entered a new phase from then on.

So when my mother and father raised the idea of moving to Lincolnshire to be near their new grandchildren, I immediately encouraged them. They arrived within that first month, following our lead and leaving London behind to move to a house just two hundred yards round the corner.

The job of settling into the community was also made much easier by the neighbours. There were only six homes there and we got on with all their occupants. A retired couple, Frank and Daisy Archer, lived next door. They helped us a lot. They had greenhouses, and a rosebush that Frank had lovingly tended for forty years. He helped me start growing vegetables. On the other side was another retired lady, Mrs Maskell; her daughter lived next door with her husband. Then there was old Mr and Mrs Barton and Mr and Mrs Nicholson who had won £4,000 on the football pools in 1948 but – according to local legend – never spent a penny of it. They 'could have bought the whole of Firsby, lock, stock and barrel', they used to joke.

The life these neighbours led was much slower than that we'd been used to in London. In fact it was comatose compared to 'the smoke' as everyone referred to it. We'd been in advertising which had been pretty crazy, everything was wanted yesterday. In Lincolnshire it was 'maybe we'll do that today'. If I'm honest, we were a little patronizing towards the place during those early days. We thought of it as backward, I suppose. I remember I used to write to relatives with dispatches from the outback, recounting in one how I'd been dive-bombed by some birds. I enjoyed sitting in the kitchen scribbling out long-winded missives. By the time I'd finished that one I'd turned Firsby into a replica of the town in Alfred Hitchcock's *The Birds*.

To anyone reading those letters it must have been crystal clear that it was going to take a long time for us to adjust to country life. If only we'd all had that time on our side . . .

Ten days or so after we'd moved in, I was in the front garden when I saw a pick-up truck pulling up at the gate. I recognized the man who climbed out as Don the farmer, whose land backed on to our garden. If I'd been expecting a friendly welcome to the community, I was soon disappointed.

Lincolnshire farmers are no different to farmers anywhere else. He didn't beat about the bush.

'Here, do you own this flippin' dog that's running riot around my livestock?' he said, leaning over the front gate.

I didn't really know how to respond but I wouldn't have had time anyway. He hadn't finished saying his piece yet. 'You bloody Londoners, you come into the country and think you can take over and let your animals run around as they like. You'd better keep her under control, or if my dogs don't get her I will – with my shotgun.'

Purdey's reaction to the countryside had been perhaps our biggest headache. Back in London she had been a lovely, inoffensive little dog. She was a touch nervous in that she would run away from people she didn't know, but otherwise she was no trouble at all.

She was a totally different character to Shane. I had lavished so much one-to-one attention on Shane. He slept on the bed with me, and when I was away from him he used to howl. He would scratch the door and whine if I was in a room out of his sight. Purdey was much more relaxed, probably down to the fact that I wasn't able to spend so much time with her because I was so busy with the children. She could relax.

But almost the moment she arrived in the countryside she went from being a happy six-month-old dog to a maniac. It was terrible.

Back in Wimbledon, she was used to having a lot of people around. She was used to traffic and trains because we had a level crossing near us. Like me, I think she found the quiet and the solitude of the countryside overwhelming.

She had run off into the fields behind the house within the first few days. The far end of the garden was an untamed wilderness and the fencing all the way around the property was inadequate so we stood little chance of keeping her in. We set off looking for her, but to no avail. Eventually she came home, agitated and breathless. We had no idea where she had been. A day or so later, it happened again. Once more we set off looking for her. Once more we had to wait for her to return under her own steam.

Given that we were trying to move into a house as well, it was a pain in the backside. It felt as if we were always asking each other: 'For goodness sake, where's she now?' And we couldn't understand why. She had a good home, we fed her well, but she just kept running off. Naively, we hadn't considered the possibility that she was up to no good during her wanderings.

Our visit from Don meant the problem was far more serious than we had realized. Tony and I had to act – and fast.

We both knew the farmer was perfectly within his rights to shoot a dog that was trespassing on his land and threatening his livelihood. We knew we had to break this habit before he carried out his threats.

At first we thought it was a question of exercise. We thought Purdey wasn't getting enough physical work and so we decided to tire her out. Tony and I began taking Purdey on epic walks. We'd ride alongside on a bicycle, while she walked mile after mile of country lane. On one occasion we took her out for three hours. By the time she arrived home she was trembling with exhaustion, her little legs were wobbling. But it didn't make any difference. We went into the kitchen for a cup of tea, turned round and she was gone again. We just looked at each other as if to say: 'What now?' Reluctantly we decided to tether her to a fifty-foot washing line so she couldn't run away. Any opportunity she had she took. Once she even went through the front window. As soon as she vanished we'd go looking for her again.

Soon everyone was being roped into the search parties. I'd go to my dad and he'd say, 'Not again.' I didn't mind the moaning, I just wanted to find her and get her home safe and well. I'd even go to the farm and sneak around to make sure she wasn't there bothering the animals. I really feared Don was going to shoot her.

I had sympathy at home, and within the family. My London family were asking why it mattered if a dog roamed, because of course there our dogs wandered the streets all the time. They didn't understand the anomaly that in London there were plenty of places to walk your dog. In the country there were next to none, because all the fields belonged to the farmers.

Predictably there was only one opinion in the community. Everyone said the dog was 'no good'. Our local vet's practice had two surgeries, one in Spilsby, the other in Skegness. Desperate to sort the problem out, I took Purdey along to be given tranquillizers to calm her down.

John Dabell, the vet on duty that day, was a typical country practitioner: corduroy trousers, tweed jacket, a big, ruddy-cheeked man. He liked large animals and looked as if he could handle them. People, however, were less of a speciality. John was not good on bedside manner. His view was this is life, deal with it. So, predictably, he had little sympathy for me. I explained what was happening. 'The poor dog's in a pickle,' I said.

'She'll be no use to you here,' he replied. 'She's neither use nor ornament.'

It put me under a lot of pressure, because I was desperate to get off to a good start in the community. I didn't want people to mark me down as a townie with no respect for the countryside. At the same time both the vet and my father were telling me this dog was totally unacceptable. My dad asked me: 'Do you want the community to hate you before you've even started?'

I didn't know what to do. It got so bad that I used to dream about Purdey. I would imagine she was down in the disused World War II airfield at the end of our road chasing rabbits instead of harassing Don's chickens.

We thought we'd got the problem under control. But then I saw Don one market day in Spilsby.

'I saw your dog out again the other day,' he said.

'I'm sorry, we're doing all we can to sort it out,' I said.

'There's only one thing that'll sort that one out and it's a bullet in the head,' he replied.

Ironically, however, Purdey's fate was sealed at home rather than on Don's farm. I have written before about the events of that autumn. It was clear that Purdey's anxiety was getting more acute. She had always been a nervous dog, now she seemed to be gripped by paranoia. And it began to manifest itself within the home, and – crucially – around the children. Two incidents brought matters to a head. First Purdey sent young Tony crashing through a glass door inside the house. It left him with a scar to his face that would remain with him for life. Then she nipped

Ellie on the face while my mother was looking after her one morning. It was the final straw. That day I reluctantly accepted my father's argument that 'Once a dog has turned that's it.'

It still haunts me that I wasn't strong enough to resist. I was twenty-four and I was being bombarded by all this negativity. If she hadn't bitten Ellie would she have lived? I don't know.

On the same morning I took her to the local vet's surgery. John Dabell was on duty once more. He tried to be as sympathetic as he could. After he had administered the injection that ended her life he said: 'You had no choice, she was a wrong 'un.'

To be honest, I was so concerned about getting back to Ellie afterwards that I didn't have time to take in the enormity of what had happened. The reaction was only delayed a few hours, however.

Once more, I lay awake in the darkness that night, listening to the sound of silence outside. Try as I might, however, I couldn't rid myself of the sense of failure I felt. I had let that poor little dog down. It was a guilt that would never fully leave me. That night I felt like I was falling off the edge of nowhere.

Chapter 9

The Good Life

In the mid-1970s everyone's favourite television programme was *The Good Life* with Felicity Kendal and
Richard Briers. It was one of those once-in-a-generation
shows that touch a nation's nerve. I remember reading how
city dwellers had started ripping up their patios and turning
their gardens into cabbage patches. I think it tapped into
a desperation to get away from the pressures of city life, a
dream to get back to nature. The enjoyment I got watching
the show came in part from knowing that we'd already
achieved that. We were living the good life for real.

Two and a half years on from our arrival in the country,
the wilderness at the back of the house had been transformed into a cross between a market garden and a farm-
yard. The weeds had been replaced by healthy, green
patches of cabbages and cauliflowers, well-tended rows of
peas and runner beans, potatoes and beetroots. The rundown sheds at the bottom of the garden had been converted
into coops and houses for our collection of chickens, ducks
and goats.

We had about a dozen animals in all. Every creature had

been given a name, of course. The children had come up with most of them – hence the strong Beatrix Potter element. The ducks were called Jeremy, Jemima, Hansel and Gretel and Mrs Tittlemouse. There was another one called Dopey, because, well, it was a bit dopey. We had two goats called Milly and Molly. Naturally, when they produced a kid it was immediately christened Mandy. As well as providing eggs and occasional milk, the animals were a wonderful source of entertainment and companionship for the children.

It had taken two and a half years to carve this life out. And in that time nothing had come easily.

Financially it had taken us months to get ourselves on our feet. Tony had spent most of the first six months on the dole. We were forced to live on £21 a week. Eventually he was offered a job at £19 a week building chalets at Butlin's in Skegness. It was a drop in money, but he needed to get back to work for his sanity and his pride. Our spirits had immediately been lifted. In some ways the leanest times of our lives were the most fun as well. Eventually he had found a job that suited his talents better, working on the sales force of a greetings card company.

Meanwhile I had carried on with the task of raising the children – and doing my Felicity Kendal impersonations in the garden. My attempts to grow our own vegetables had been a mixed success, to say the least. Part of the problem was that I hadn't wanted to use pesticides. I wanted our produce to be healthy, unpolluted. This was long before the word organic had entered everyday parlance. But I soon discovered why pesticides had been produced in the first place. That summer I watched our crop of sweetcorn blossom spectacularly. But when the moment came to remove the husks, we found the birds had got there before us. Our cauliflowers suffered too. The first crop were no bigger than the new fifty-pence pieces. I left the radishes in the ground too long and discovered they were as hard and inedible as wood.

I did my best to overcome the problems. I built a variety of scary mechanisms to frighten off the birds, tying bits of rag to poles to flap in the winds.

In the meantime I was transformed into something I never thought I'd become, a real 'earth mother' making jams and cooking pies, bread and rainbow puddings for the kids.

My mother, of course, used it as a justification for the way she'd raised me. 'I told you those cookery lessons would come in useful,' she said one day.

By then I was immune to her little digs. I was, I will admit, revelling in it. It will sound pathetic now but one of the proudest moments of my life came when one evening I produced the first meal entirely derived from our own garden. It wasn't exactly cordon bleu cookery, but to us it was a meal fit for royalty – fried duck eggs and chips made from our own, garden-grown potatoes. I can't ever remember relishing a meal so much.

As I became used to the pace of life, I had learned to appreciate my surroundings too. Lincolnshire and its countryside had slowly cast its spell.

I would walk with the children into Spilsby, putting the shopping under the pram. Because it was so quiet the animals were all around us. You would see rabbits, foals, horses, goats, all sorts of birds and of course lots of sheep and cows. I found myself getting up early in the morning to go for walks before the children and Tony were up. I remember seeing my first badger and fox on those early morning strolls. It was like meeting the cast of *Watership Down*.

We were also more aware of the weather and the seasons.

In London, there were only two main types of weather during my childhood – hot and sticky or foggy. The most memorable aspect of nature I saw were the infamous 'pea soupers', fogs so thick they turned the air a dull, dark orange, made your eyes water and forced you to cover up your mouth for fear of choking on the vile-tasting atmosphere. The last of them had been in December 1962, when my Nan Whitton died. I remember my father trying to drive through the streets of Fulham as we headed to the undertaker, and my mother with her head stuck out of the window shouting instructions as we felt our way, inch by inch, along the road. 'There's the kerb, Wal, be careful.'

In Lincolnshire, it was as if I was seeing the turning of the seasons for the first time. I watched the corn turn golden in the fields, the trees blossoming each spring, the fall of the leaves in autumn. I had probably seen some of these things in London, but they had never registered. Now they were things to be appreciated, signs of the wonder of life in the English landscape.

For the first time too I found myself looking at the world through my Nan Fennell's eyes. I would watch the skies and the sunsets in particular. The colours were amazing. Our house faced due west so we saw some phenomenal sunsets. I used to look forward to the evenings and the vivid hues that would form on the horizon. It was then that I understood for the first time what sky blue pink meant.

Our happiness in Firsby was increased by the fact that we now felt part of the community. The troubles we'd had with Purdey hadn't exactly got us off on the right foot with the locals. With some justification, they had probably marked us down as hapless townies. No one ever said it to me, but they probably expected to see us heading back down the A1 to London within the first year.

If there had been a turning point, it had probably come during the area's darkest hour.

As I drew back the curtains one winter morning, it was no great surprise to see the sky filled with steely grey clouds. The rain had been drumming on our window pane all night. What was something of a shock, however, was the sight of Kelpie our new gundog's kennel floating on what looked like a miniature lake in the back garden. Through the downpour, I could make out the sound of her barking for help.

Lincolnshire's infamously flat landscape is criss-crossed with a network of dykes. We didn't know it when we moved there but the low-lying land is prone to flooding. Two dykes extended along the full length of Eastfield Road, one either side of the lane. We had to cross over a deep ditch by means of a small footpath to reach our front garden.

The dykes had proven no match for the downpour. As I jumped down the staircase I saw that we were flooded. The house was a muddied mess. Downstairs, chairs and toys were bobbing around in the brown water. A rotten smell already filled the air. The creeping dampness was climbing up the walls and the curtains. It was horrible and heartbreaking to behold.

Fortunately, the community was already – literally – lending all hands to the pump. Some of the older people had seen this before and seemed to know instinctively what to do. They were already laying sandbags in place. Soon they were helping us shift our furniture upstairs before it was completely ruined.

I'd seen this community spirit at work once before. During our second winter we were snowed in by the worst storm I'd ever encountered.

The snow had begun falling heavily the night before. But we still weren't prepared for the sight that greeted us the next morning.

Because Lincolnshire is so flat, when the winds come the snow just banks up. It was twenty feet deep, deeper in some places. In some places it was a few inches, but a few yards away it was twelve feet deep. In Holton Holgate there was a dip into Great Steeping; nobody could get through, it was banked up so deeply.

At first we didn't consider the possibility that we were marooned. Old Mr Barton said: 'Don't worry. Don the farmer's got through before on his tractor and he'll do it again this time.' Everyone seemed quite relaxed about it. Until, that is, someone heard on the radio that a snow-plough had been lost on the way down from Spilsby. That's when we realized we were in for a long wait. Adversity brought out the best in the place, however. Everyone pulled together. The younger people went out to do the physical work, clearing the snow off the paths and the road while the older ones stayed indoors rustling up soup and lighting fires.

After a few hours Don did get through. He and his wife brought round fresh supplies of milk for anyone who needed it. With two young children, needless to say it was manna from heaven for me.

I'd heard my mother talk about the amazing camaraderie and community spirit that London saw during the Blitz. Now she really responded, she was in her element. In all we were snowed in for three days. By the end of it, our neighbours seemed like our closest friends in the world. So I wasn't surprised at the spirit that was shown during the floods.

Talking to the neighbours I discovered that this had been a problem off and on over many years. The Water Board had talked before about dealing with the situation, but had done nothing. They were equally ineffectual this time. The waters only receded after the fire brigade dug up the road to relieve the flooding, leaving us to get on with the mopping-up operation. It took us weeks to get straight again and such was the anger at the way the Water Board had failed to react to an obvious problem that we collectively complained.

Reluctantly – very reluctantly – the officials agreed to compensate us. Everyone was satisfied with this. But it soon became apparent that the Water Board were in no hurry to pay up. Days turned into weeks, weeks into months. We were all getting miffed about the situation.

Then one day, I was listening to the newly launched local BBC radio station, Radio Lincolnshire. Someone from the Water Board was being interviewed. Sounding holier-than-thou, he was claiming that part of the problem was the fact that people didn't pay their water rates.

I got on the phone immediately and let rip on the air. I've always had to speak out when things were wrong. I paid my water rates and I was sure everyone else in our road did as well. That was no excuse to withhold our compensation. I was livid. I had never been one to write angry letters to the newspapers but for a few minutes I became 'Disgusted of Firsby'.

Everyone was listening to the new station at the time, so the community heard me. I wasn't expecting to be slapped on the back for saying what I'd said, but at the same time I didn't expect the reaction I got either. Our neighbours were not confrontational types. They weren't the sort of people to have a go at someone in public. But there was no doubting what they were thinking. Loud-mouthed Londoner probably summed it up. To judge from the way they avoided me over the following few days I had instantly been transformed into public enemy number one. Everyone clearly assumed that I had ruined our chances of ever receiving compensation.

It wasn't long afterwards, however, that I got a call from the radio station asking if they could come down and do a longer interview with me about the problems we'd been having.

Somehow news of this got back to the Water Board. They were soon on the phone themselves.

The gist of their call was immediately made clear. If you don't go ahead with the interview we'll pay up in full.

I asked for a promise of this in writing, which duly arrived. We got our cheques shortly before Christmas.

Again, no one said anything directly to me. But the smiles I received out and about over the holiday season spoke volumes.

There's an old saying in the countryside that you're only a local if there are three generations of your family in the graveyard. I couldn't claim that, nor would I ever be able to. But during my time in Firsby, that was the moment when I really felt part of the place.

Chapter 10

Soft Touch

If there was one aspect of my new life that continued to make me feel uncomfortable it was the harshness of the countryside. In Lincolnshire animals were seen as expendable, working creatures whose lives were somehow less valuable than ours. There was no place for sentimentality. I understood why it had to be this way. Farming was, after all, a business, not a hobby. But it still remained a philosophy I found it hard to share – no matter how hard I tried.

One evening during our second year in Lincolnshire, Tony had started talking about the logical next step in our drive to be self-sufficient. Hunting was, we both agreed, a natural extension of what we were doing with the garden and the poultry. The occasional rabbit, pheasant or partridge would be a welcome addition to the kitchen, we thought. The idea that I would be involved even indirectly in hunting would have been unimaginable when I lived in London. It was a measure of how hard I was trying to fit into the new environment.

It quickly dawned on me what the next step would be.

Late in 1973, we welcomed a new addition to the home: Kelpie, our gundog. In many ways Kelpie was a symbol of the progress I'd made in putting our bad start behind us.

The trauma of Purdey had affected me deeply. I thought about her a lot. 'Get on with it,' I told myself repeatedly when I became tearful, which was often. For a while I'd sworn that I would never have another dog again in my life. I was still convinced I was bad luck.

Of course, the minute Tony's new hunting assistant arrived at the house I thought: 'Yes, this dog belongs here.' All the old feelings flooded back. It seemed right.

Kelpie came from near Boston, and was a working bred English springer spaniel. She was a tiny little puppy, a diddy liver and white thing. We felt sure that we were not going to get a reprise of the problems we had with Purdey.

Tony was determined to train his gundog by the traditional method. He had been given no shortage of advice by his hunting pals. Some of it made me furious.

I realized then that there is more violence doled out in the gundog world than anywhere else in canine circles. A farmer who lived in a village near us had a dog that always looked terrified. He used to drive around in a pick-up truck. Every time he looked at the dog it cringed. His philosophy was that you should let a gundog run amok for eighteen months, then beat it to within an inch of its life. That way it would respect you for ever. It was not an uncommon view.

Tony thankfully ignored that, but I still had qualms about the route he was being advised to take. To be fair, it accorded with the best-respected dog experts of the day.

The books recommended that the dog needed to live outside the house, isolated so that it only had a relationship with its master. The theory was that this way the dog would be ready to obey its master's commands when out on the hunt and wouldn't be distracted by anyone else.

This went strongly against my better instincts, I have to admit. It didn't compute to me. If a dog is kept in a kennel and run for six days of the week, on the seventh day it isn't going to be much use on the hunt because it hasn't had any exercise. But I wasn't going to interfere. Tony built a kennel and run outside and that's where Kelpie lived – for a while at least.

It was close to Christmas when the first really wild weather hit us. Early in the evening we heard Kelpie's plaintive yelping. She was clearly cold, lonely and desperate to join us in the warmth of the house. Tony kept going out to the window. He could see Kelpie who looked tiny and pathetic. He was only doing what he had been told, of course. You don't pamper gundogs. Each time he came away he said: 'She's got to learn, she's got to learn.' But every time he said it he seemed less convinced.

I watched him crumpling, at one point I could see him with his fingers in his ears. By about half past ten that night he had given in. 'I think I'll let her in for a little while,' he said. That was the end of her outdoor exile. From that night on she slept in the house with us. And it didn't make her any worse as a gundog.

To those who had spent all their lives in the country, my queasiness about the grim realities of life was a source of quiet amusement. One memory in particular still makes me blush with embarrassment.

I went into the garden early one morning to be greeted by a distressing sight. One of the ducks, Jemima, was lying prostrate on the grass. It was quivering and was clearly in a lot of distress. I'm no ornithologist, but I saw immediately that it had broken its back. Realizing there was no alternative, I wrapped the little thing up in a towel, put it in the car and headed for the vet's surgery in Spilsby.

Since arriving in Lincolnshire I had formed two very different relationships with our duo of practising vets, John Dabell and Josh Cooper. John's reaction to putting down Purdey summed him up. He loved and respected animals, of that I was in absolutely no doubt. But he had the countryman's view of their place in the scheme of things. Purdey had been out of control, and in the countryside there was no room for a dog like that. I'd seen him regularly over the years I'd been in Firsby, and he never tired of telling me I'd have to 'harden up', as he put it.

To be fair to him, I had provided plenty of evidence to support his view that I was a soft touch.

At one point we'd had a problem with Kelpie, I recall. She'd hurt herself while out working one day. Back at home she was wincing and couldn't lift her head. When John came to see her he told us she'd probably pulled a muscle or dislocated a vertebra. He prescribed painkillers and told me to give her plenty of rest. For the rest of the day she lay on the sofa where I had propped her head up with a pillow.

This went on for a week or more and there was no improvement. John was puzzled by this. He was sure she shouldn't still need painkillers. But I told him how Kelpie whined and cried whenever I tried to move her. She lay there lapping up the sympathy, we'd lift her up and carry her to the toilets. We'd plump the pillows up for her.

Back in those days country vets really were figures straight from a James Herriot novel. They'd make house calls on request and often pop in just for a cup of tea and a piece of cake. One day John called in to see us in the middle of his rounds. While he was there I heard the sound of miaowing. It was coming from a basket that I saw contained three kittens. Naive as ever, I asked, 'What's wrong with them?'

John gave me a dismissive look and said, 'You don't want to know.' Someone had clearly asked him to dispose of them.

'Can I have one?' I asked.

He was caught by surprise but after a moment's reflection said: 'Yup, why not?'

When John left, I walked into the sitting room and put the kitten on the floor. It was then that the miracle occurred. Like Lazarus rising from the dead, Kelpie leapt off the sofa, licked the kitten, rolled it over and started playing with it. When Tony came home he saw Kelpie transformed and exclaimed: 'What's happened?'

'It's called Jimmy,' I said.

There was Kelpie and the kitten lying in front of the fire. She'd been playing us for mugs, milking us.

When I told John about this he laughed. Inadvertently he'd provided the cure, of course. But he took it as an opportunity to remind me of his view of me. 'Any dog would be able to string you along, you're a soft touch,' he said.

Josh, on the other hand, was a real dog lover. Part of me was hoping it would be Josh that was on duty when I arrived with the duck. I discovered it was John. He stifled a smile when I walked into the surgery cradling a duck. He must have thought: 'I've seen it all now.' Normally he was the most straight-talking of men. But, on this occasion, he kept his thoughts to himself. I asked him to put the duck down. He nodded, still half-smiling. 'I'll do that for you, yes,' he said. He confirmed my diagnosis that it was a broken back. 'No option, is there?' he said.

He did the job in his usual quick and efficient way. He was a big man, but there was a tenderness about him when it came to animals. As I watched him administer the injection, I couldn't help thinking: 'It's awful work but somebody's got to do it.'

With the duck put out of its misery, he told me he'd dispose of the body. I asked him how much.

It was then that a gentle smile broke out across his face. 'Fifty pence,' he said.

'Sorry?' I replied.

'Fifty pence,' he said again.

I burst out into a grin as well. I understood what he was saying. Who else but me would have brought a duck to his surgery? A farmer would have wrung the poor animal's neck without a second thought.

There would always be a dark, brutal aspect to the countryside that I didn't like. To be honest, I didn't want to know about it. I knew there were certain farming practices that I violently disapproved of. But at the same time,

I respected the farmers' right to earn a living and appreciated that, for a lot of them, that was a really hard job.

I think that's when John realized I was never going to see the world as men like him did. I wasn't going to harden up.

Even more significant that day, however, was that there was no malice or disdain in his reaction. He knew animals were at the centre of both our lives. We simply had different philosophies about how to live with them. Somewhere in those exchanged smiles we came to an understanding of each other.

Chapter 11

Circle of Friends

As I immersed myself more and more in country life, the days when dogs were my secret friendships seemed an ever more distant memory.

It had been John Dabell who had first planted the idea of breeding a litter of dogs. When I'd first taken Kelpie for a booster jab, he'd taken an instant shine to her. 'This is more like it,' he'd said, referring back to poor Purdey. 'You should breed from this one, she's a lovely dog.' As it turned out, Kelpie was unable to conceive when we tried mating her with another dog in Norwich. And soon after that she left us.

Tony's work commitments meant that he now had no time for shooting. And Kelpie had found it hard to adjust to the arrival of a new dog, Lady.

The idea of getting a springer for myself had taken root when we went to Norwich with Kelpie. The owner of the kennels there had a beautiful showdog and it had set me thinking about getting one and trying my own hand in the competitive arena. I began researching the breed through the Kennel Club. They recommended me to a springer society who then put me in contact with a woman in Barnet, north London. I travelled down and paid 35 guineas for a lovely puppy. I named her Lady after the imaginary dog of my childhood.

Lady was a remarkable dog, a creature with real presence and energy. I learned early on that I had to be very careful whenever I brought Lady to see Josh Cooper. She'd taken a real shine to him almost immediately, so much so that as soon as she heard him calling for us from the surgery she'd bolt into his room and jump all over him and his desk. On more than one occasion she'd sent instruments and paperwork flying everywhere. To avert any more disasters like this Josh had got into the habit of ushering me in silently.

Lady was such a character that she became the first dog I took to shows. We made our debut early in 1976 at a small, monthly 'match' meeting held by the Lincoln Canine Society. To my delight Lady won a pink rosette for Best Puppy Walk. It felt like I'd won a gold medal at the Olympics.

It was as if I'd opened a door on a new aspect of life. I really enjoyed it, not least because of the camaraderie and general sociability the dog world seemed to engender. Lady and I soon started travelling around the Midlands and the North of England, competing in the 'exemption shows'. At one show I'd got talking to Jean Sheppard, a leading light in the springer world. She'd told me that if I wanted to see the best of the breed I should go to a big champion-ship show held in Loughborough, Leicestershire every April. I went along and was bowled over by the beauty and personality of the dogs I saw there. From then on, springers were the breed that held a special place in my affections.

To my surprise, Lady began picking up prizes on a regular basis. They were generally fourth or fifth places, but they all counted. By November 1975, we had a key qualifying event for Cruft's, the Midland English Springer Spaniel Society meeting at Wakefield in Yorkshire. By now Lady was eleven months old. She competed in the Puppy Bitch class for dogs six to twelve months old. I must admit that by now I was beginning to get the feel of the competition arena. And Lady too had really come to enjoy it. As we took part in the competition in Wakefield she was up against fourteen or fifteen other dogs. But she wasn't at all fazed and showed really nicely, wagging her tail and being very enthusiastic as I put her through her paces. When the judge came to his decision he placed her first. We won a cup, but far more importantly we were off to Cruft's.

A few months later, in April 1976, we headed down to London and the famous arena at Olympia, on my old stamping ground in west London. The sights and sounds of the North End Road and Olympia took me back to my days with Shane. It was strange being there with another dog, but a thrill to be among so many wonderful examples of the canine world. Even though Cruft's had been staged down the road from where we lived, I'd never been anywhere near the place until now. The closest I'd been to it had been watching *Blue Peter*'s coverage on television as a child. It was a thrilling sight.

I was really excited about the competition – a little too excited, truth be told. Lady was entered in the 'special junior' category. We registered and made ourselves ready for the big moment, then marched into the famous arena with the rest of the dogs in the class. It was as I looked up at the massed ranks of people staring down at us that things began to go wrong. I will never forget the feeling that suddenly swept over me. It wasn't just a case of butterflies, it was sheer, screaming terror. I started shaking like a leaf and felt physically sick.

The instruction came to start showing the dogs, but by now I was a gibbering wreck. And of course Lady picked up on this. As I fidgeted and fussed over her, she too began to get wound up. When it came to our turn to move around the arena we were all at sea. We had practised walking together for hour after hour at home. I was conscious of the banks of people – knowledgeable dog people – looking down at me. I was convinced they were laughing to each other, sure they must have been whispering: 'Look at those two, how the hell did they let them in here?'

I'd become very friendly with a well-known couple in that close-knit community, Bert and Gwen Green. When the judge put us out of our misery and awarded all the prizes to other dogs, I met Bert outside the arena. He was a very straightforward chap. 'If you'd shaken much more your head would have dropped off,' he joked. But then he put a fatherly arm on my shoulder and set it all in perspective. 'You'll be back,' he said. 'Look on this as your apprenticeship.'

It took me a while to get over the disappointment, and it was Bert and Gwen who helped revive my spirits. I'd mentioned to them that I'd like to start breeding. They called me one day saying they had a dog they thought would be perfect as a 'foundation bitch' for me. The fact that she was family made her even more appealing. The dog was Donna, Lady's three-year-old 'grandmother'. Donna was a commanding character, one of those dogs whose charisma follows them into a room. I quickly nick-named her The Duchess.

I didn't want to become one of those people who pump out dogs as if they were commodities at a factory. But at the same time I did like the idea of producing pedigree dogs. Donna provided me with the first litter of puppies. I kept one of them, Chrissy, for myself and gave the rest to reputable dog owners. Chrissy was a very successful showdog. He won a puppy class at the age of eight months and qualified for Cruft's too. The highlight of my time with him came in October 1977 when I took him to the Show Spaniels Field Day, a prestigious event for working dogs qualified for Cruft's. The competition judged the dogs on their working ability as well as their looks. Chrissy won the prize for Best English Springer on the Day. The memories of Cruft's the previous year were already con-signed to history.

Dogs meant much more to me than rosettes and champion-ship cups. And it was during this time that I was reminded of the power they have to heal and lift the spirits.

By now, we had made such a great life for ourselves that I really felt we should share it with people less fortunate than we were. So we applied to become foster parents and were accepted by the local social services department. Over a period of three years or so we fostered six or seven children. I really enjoyed being able to give those children the things that – for whatever reason – their families were temporarily unable to provide.

They would arrive and fit into our lives. The only thing I insisted on was that we never took any children older than Tony and Ellie. I didn't want an older child influencing them.

No one needed to persuade me about the power dogs have to bring good into people's lives. But there were plenty of others who didn't see it. Donna and Lady showed one of the social workers just how great an influence they could be when we fostered two lovely little boys, Darren and Jamie.

They lived with their mother, but she had been taken ill and was in hospital. With no one else to look after them they had been put in care. We were asked whether we would take them until their mother recovered.

Social services had been pleased with the work we'd done with the few children we'd had. The social worker who brought the two boys to us had one reservation: the dogs. She wondered whether they might be a danger to the boys. I said: 'Quite the opposite.' But she didn't believe me.

I was told that Darren was missing his mother badly and wasn't very communicative. He hadn't said a word during the ten days he had been in care. That changed the moment he arrived at our house. And it was down to the dogs.

The two boys walked in together. When Darren saw Donna and Lady his eyes lit up like a Christmas tree.

'Doggy,' he said, beaming.

During the time he was with us his speech came along

in leaps and bounds. But everything he said was connected to the dogs. If he saw one of them playing with the ball it was: 'Doggy got ball.' If they were eating it was: 'Doggy eat dinner.' Two days after Darren and Jamie had arrived the same social worker came back to see how we were getting on. She was amazed at how relaxed Darren was and even more incredulous that he was speaking.

'How did you do it?' she asked me.

'I didn't,' I replied, looking over at Donna and Lady. 'Those two did.'

I was taken aback one day in the summer of 1978, when I was approached by a lady who ran a kennel in the area.

Her name was Sheila Glover and I had met her originally through the Lincoln and Boston Canine Society, of which we were both members.

She told me she was thinking about starting an obedience class at Firsby. 'It's going to be too much work for one person, I wondered whether you'd be willing to help me,' she said.

'You'd be great,' she added, clearly sensing my inner thoughts. 'Talk about the blind leading the blind,' I'd started saying to myself.

As it happened, I had been taking more and more interest in training dogs, mainly because I had acquired some new members of my own pack.

Tragically Donna had died of a tumour, aged only eight, but in the aftermath I had taken in two cocker spaniels for the children, Susie and her daughter Sandy. I had also started thinking about the implications of breeding. The fact that I was breeding dogs that would be sold on to homes as pets meant I had a responsibility. It was up to me to make sure the puppies that left my care were well-trained, well-behaved dogs. For this reason I agreed to Sheila's idea and set about advertising it with her over the coming weeks.

We booked the Firsby Village Hall and one evening, after the girl guides had finished their get-together, launched our inaugural class.

It was a measure of how dog-orientated the area was that we got a very healthy turn-out from the beginning. There must have been a dozen to twenty owners there.

In small, subtle ways I'd begun to soften the more aggressive elements of traditional training. For instance I tried as much as possible to avoid so-called choke chains. And when I did turn to them I tried to change people's attitude by calling them check chains. But as we got the course going I stuck to the traditional textbooks. I was afraid to do anything else. The memory of poor Purdey was never far from my mind. And I was determined that I was never going to let something like that happen again if I could help it.

As a result of the classes I gained something of a reputation among local dog people. At one point I was approached by a local family who were having trouble with a pair of highly exuberant Bouviers de Flandres called Ziggy and Benson.

They asked me to take the pair in for a fortnight so as to improve their behaviour. I remember they paid me £15 a week – but in truth I achieved very little. As Ziggy and Benson bounded around my own house much as they had done around their owners' I was asking myself all the right questions. Why aren't they taking any notice of me? Shouldn't this training be happening within an environment where there's a chance they are going to be relaxed, i.e. their home? The only problem was I didn't have any answers. I felt a bit of a fraud for taking the money.

My – undeserved – reputation as a dog expert spread further too.

By now I was working as a home help and through a friend had agreed to assist a Miss Vincent. She lived near Skegness and owned a black cocker spaniel called Henry, who would bite her whenever she attempted to trim his coat.

Cocker spaniels' coats are very silky and can get knotted up easily even if they are being brushed regularly. Henry was so ferocious you couldn't trim his coat; it was so matted and woolly you couldn't even comb it. Miss Vincent was covered in bites, and other people who had tried to groom him had also been attacked. The only way we could manage was for the vet to give the dog an anaesthetic, so that I could cut his whole coat off while he was asleep. We'd have to do this every two months. I used to dread Miss Vincent's phone call.

On one occasion John Dabell came to put Henry out. After he had administered the injection, we sat in the kitchen with Miss Vincent watching Henry continue to growl at us. A full dose of anaesthetic hadn't worked. The poor dog's coat was all matted and Miss Vincent couldn't go near him. I spoke to John but he said: 'I can't give him another, it will kill him.'

So I had to tell Miss Vincent I couldn't help her any

117

more. In the end she said: 'I think I'll have to have Henry put to sleep.' This was far from uncommon in those days. People routinely wrote off entire breeds of dogs as being aggressive and cocker spaniels were among the worst victims.

Henry was only two. Josh Cooper was given the unenviable task of putting him to sleep. I was there that day to support Miss Vincent through her ordeal. I watched Josh carry the black bag containing poor Henry out to the van.

As I looked at Henry's body lying in the back of the car, the questions began to pile up as they had with Ziggy and Benson. I kept thinking, why? Why was he like this? Why did he react to people helping him? It was another turning point. It affected me badly, it really upset me. Henry died, I know now, because of our ignorance. He was another dog who paid the price for our lack of understanding.

One night, six months or so after we'd begun the obedience classes, the doors to the village hall swung violently open. In bounded a huge, bull mastiff-like mongrel. Hanging on for grim life in a pair of leather gloves that were presumably to protect her hands from rope burns was his owner, a slight, middle-aged lady. She didn't need to open her mouth. Every inch of her being was shouting out the message: 'Help.' Somewhere inside me the same thoughts immediately began bubbling away.

As the classes had gone on I had gained some confidence. Deep down, however, I'd begun to see that we weren't making a huge difference. Our method was a watered-down, less aggressive version of what Barbara Woodhouse, the television personality, was doing at the time; in other words, traditional obedience. It was all harsh instructions and stern rebukes for dogs that deigned to disobey their master. Even if it had worked I wouldn't have liked it.

Far too many dogs would behave perfectly during the class; then, the minute their owners clipped on their lead and led them to the doors, they would haul them away again. I felt that we were muddling through and had already said as much to Sheila.

The moment I set eyes on this dog, I knew we were in trouble.

The lady paid her twenty pence and joined the class. Her dog was so big and boisterous that I had to deal with him first. So I asked her to bring him to the centre of the hall where I began to apply the same old, traditional methods I'd been using since the class began. We got the other dogs to walk around him in an attempt to make him feel at home but he was having none of it. We then tried to persuade him to sit and stay. I spent fifteen minutes or so getting nowhere. Sheila took over, trying to elicit some sort of positive response, but to no avail.

Throughout, the dog had retained the same aggressive expression. It looked fit to kill. Someone whispered to me, 'This dog is evil.' I didn't think I was capable of agreeing with such sentiments – but for a few moments I found I was nodding quietly to myself.

We had been doing this for half an hour or so when the dog's owner jumped into the middle of the hall. Sheila and I had both issued the dog with increasingly desperate dressing downs. I think one of us had gone up close to him and said 'Bad dog' at one point. This had clearly been too much for the owner.

'Stop it, stop it, you're bullying my dog,' she said indignantly. She was crying.

Sheila and I were speechless.

'I'm never coming here again. Call yourselves experts?' she said as she gathered her dog's leash in her hand once more and marched him towards the door.

As I watched her go my heart sank – mainly because I knew she was absolutely right. I realized we were out of our depth. The truth was we didn't have a clue what we were doing. And what was worse, rather than doing any good we were probably doing dogs like this harm.

As we brought the class to a close that night and tidied up the hall, I was already coming to a decision. I rang Sheila when I got home.

'I don't feel I have the right to be standing in the middle of that hall,' I told her. 'It's wrong.'

Sheila tried to talk me round but in her heart I think she knew it too. The classes carried on for a short time afterwards, but I took no part in them. As far as I was concerned, my brief career as a dog trainer was over.

Chapter 12

A Carnival of Animals

Lincolnshire and its coast was a magnet for colourful characters, but there were few more colourful than Roy Clarke.

He was a small, pugnacious man, a real pocket dynamo, with hod-carrier shoulders, no neck and stubby, cocktail sausage fingers. Whenever I see that wonderful actor Bob Hoskins I'm reminded of him.

He had been operating a small zoo under the pier in Skegness for a few months when I came across him.

By now I was doing my best to involve myself in the community. I had joined the local branch of the St John's Ambulance and had agreed to promote their work in the annual Skegness carnival that summer. We were sharing a float with the town's football club, whom Tony knew well. For some reason, we'd roped Roy and his zoo into the act as well. So for a period of a few weeks, I spent a bit of time planning the float with him.

Some people regarded him disapprovingly. The authorities eventually objected to the way he kept his collection of animals. The problem was the smallness of the cages he used rather than the conditions. He was someone who cared deeply for animals and he looked after his menagerie of monkeys, lions, snakes, toucans and bears admirably.

As I spent time with him I formed a deep regard for him. And he taught me a lot.

Early on, for instance, he'd invited me into the cage in which he kept his magnificent three-year-old lioness, Leone. The idea of being in the same space as such a ferocious animal made me feel uneasy, to say the least. But Roy's advice was spot on. The key thing was that the lion must not believe I was prey, he told me. 'Convince her that you're not vulnerable, make her believe you're not intimidated,' he counselled me quietly. To my amazement Leone gave me a cursory, almost dismissive look up and down then turned around and got on with her business. It was a lesson I would never forget.

Something else he had drummed into me, however, was the unpredictability of animals. I remember once I was there when a woman got a little too close to a bear he had in a cage. The signs were large and unmistakable in their message. 'Bears Are Unpredictable – Keep Your Distance'. But she chose to ignore it. She was carrying a handbag. Before she knew what had happened the bear had reached out a paw and ripped the bag out of her grip. She was lucky he didn't remove her entire arm, such was the ferocity and force of his movement. But it was during the carnival that I got the most memorable lesson in animal unpredictability.

For company on the float we were putting together, Roy chose a cockateel, a red-tail Indian boa constrictor and a lion cub, called 'Skeggy'. Roy told me they'd make a good combination, a blend of the comical, the cuddly and the slightly scary. 'The children will love it,' he told me.

The day of the carnival was one of the hottest of that summer. The sky was a flawless blue and the sun beat down from early that morning. I remember the road was shimmering and the sands of the beach glistened a dazzling white. The procession began sedately enough. There were huge crowds at the seaside that day and they thronged the roads leading to the esplanade where the main route lay.

Roy was on board with me. While he kept an eye on Skeggy, his daughter Tina was supposed to look after the snake. No sooner had we set off than the cockateel became agitated. Tina immediately set off to deal with it, passing the boa to me as she went. 'Here you are, Jan, look after this one,' she said nonchalantly, as if it was something I'd been doing all my life.

I must admit I hadn't been wild about the idea of being in close proximity to a large snake in the first place. In my naiveté I'd thought the snake was harmless. It was only eighteen months old, after all. Roy quickly put me straight. He shouted over instructions on how to hold the boa. The one piece of advice he rammed home to me was that I shouldn't let it coil itself around my fingers or anywhere to which its powerful grip could do any damage.

It wasn't as unpleasant as it might have been to hold. And as we set off the boa was well behaved. I had it draped across my shoulders with its head and tail stretching out on to my arms on either side. To the watching crowds, it probably looked impressive.

I heard later that my mother had been standing on the sea front looking perplexed as I went by. 'Why has Janice got a rope in her hand?' she'd asked my father. 'It's not a rope, Nona, it's a snake,' he replied. She nearly fainted apparently.

It wasn't long before I realized the snake was becoming livelier than it should have been. I had it coiled over my shoulder and felt it slithering ever so slightly. Roy's warning about not letting it coil itself around my hand was at the forefront of my mind. It tried to do this a couple of times but I managed to slip my hand out of its grip. This game of cat and mouse went on for fully ten minutes before the boa realized it wasn't getting anywhere and gave up. Suddenly it was completely lifeless. For a moment I thought it had died in the perishing heat. But in fact it had fallen asleep – probably through boredom. I thought my worries were over and I could concentrate on enjoying the parade. No chance.

As we moved slowly through the crowds, I looked down to see that Roy had been drawn into the throng and had let the lion cub's leash loosen. Skeggy was now manoeuvring herself into a position near the snake. I guessed immediately what she was planning to do. She had identified her lunch. The boa was heavy and getting heavier each minute it hung around my neck, but I managed to move it out of the lion's way. This didn't put Skeggy off, however. She was soon sniffing around again on my other side.

I spent the remainder of the procession trying to separate the lion cub from the snake. There were hundreds of people on the streets. Goodness knows what they were thinking as I passed by, ducking and diving around the tightly packed platform. I remember thinking to myself: 'I know the procession is meant to provide the holiday crowds with entertainment but this is ridiculous.' With the intense heat, I was sweating and feeling faint. But I knew I had to keep going or else there'd be hell to pay. The procession continued for an hour. I was close to exhaustion when I got off the float and the sight of Roy taking charge of his animals and loading them back into his van was one of the most welcome sights I'd ever seen.

We won the cup for the best float and I was able to make a generous contribution to the St John's Ambulance coffers. A photograph of me wrestling with the boa constrictor appeared in that week's newspaper. But it marked my only involvement with the Skegness Carnival, and the last time I worked with the more unpredictable members of the animal kingdom.

As for Roy, his brief stay in Skegness came to an end soon afterwards. It was only a few weeks later, towards the end of summer, that I went back to the pier hoping to see him. But I found the place deserted, the cages empty. It was as if it had never existed. If it hadn't been for the newspaper clipping, I'd have written the whole episode off as a product of my overactive imagination.

Chapter 13

A Broken Dream

Outside, a bitterly cold wind was driving banks of leaden clouds across the skies. Inside the house that early spring afternoon the atmosphere was just as overcast. Downstairs Tony was gathering together the last of his belongings and readying himself to make his way out to the car. I was upstairs fending off the tears, unable to watch him walk out the door.

No one who has been through a moment like that in their lives forgets the date. It was 16 March 1981, the day when the long, slow, painful process that was the breakdown of our marriage came to a conclusion.

I do not intend to get into the blame game. Mine was not the first marriage to break down, nor will it be the last. Who is to say why or when things started to fall apart? They just did. Our lives today are so complex that things happen. I know I made mistakes. I'm sure Tony feels that way too. It will do neither of us any good to rake over the ashes now. The time for argument is over.

What was not in dispute, however, was that we had been building up to this point for many months. There was no one moment that precipitated the break-up. Relationships don't end overnight, they unravel over time. Of course there had been flashpoints, arguments and moments of anger. The atmosphere between us had deteriorated to such an extent that I'd asked Tony to leave. He'd agreed to stay with a friend who lived nearby. In theory it was the beginning of a trial separation. In reality, as far as I was concerned at least, I knew it was the end. That day we were administering the last rites.

When I think back to that day I remember looking out at the steely, threatening skies and feeling as if the clouds were closing in on me. I already sensed that the future was going to be harsh and unpredictable. That soon seemed like the understatement of the year.

Tony's car pulled off at around 2 p.m. During those first few hours alone in the house, I tried desperately to keep myself busy, to drown out the thoughts in my head with the day-to-day minutiae of household life. Housework had never been one of my passions. That day – and for many a day afterwards – I was a whirling dervish around the kitchen and the house. The place had never been so spotless.

The children were my main lifeline.

I may no longer have been a wife, but I remained a mother. At the time Tony and Ellie were eleven and nine – too old to have failed to notice the deterioration in our relationship, yet too young to really appreciate what was happening. We had tried telling them of our decision. We'd tried to explain that Mummy and Daddy loved them very much but that they couldn't live together any more. Of course, it hadn't really sunk in.

When they came home from school that afternoon they

were both subdued. I tried to carry on as if nothing unusual had happened, serving up their tea and getting on with the routine of homework and bedtime. I've often been accused of being something of a Pollyanna, of seeing the world through rose-tinted spectacles. I was never more guilty of it than that day. The fact that we didn't really acknowledge their father's departure somehow convinced me the problem didn't exist. For a brief period I told myself things were going to be all right, that the children were going to adapt with ease to this huge upheaval in their life. They're resilient creatures, I told myself. What a fool.

Predictably, the tears came at bedtime. It was one of the hardest things imaginable not to cry along with them. But I didn't. Instead I tried to convince them the world was going to be all right: 'It's not the awful place you think it is right now.' It was 'Mummy's here', me jollying things along. Then I came downstairs and the floodgates opened.

The first night set the pattern for the days, weeks and months ahead. By day I would keep it together as best I could for the children, then, by night, I would drive myself close to madness trying to work out where my life had gone wrong.

Nobody escapes a divorce without a lot of soul-searching. I kept going over in my mind what had happened. One of the biggest questions was how our dreams had been smashed in this way. We had worked so hard to establish a life for ourselves in Lincolnshire. We had travelled so far in fitting into the community and overcoming our far from promising start. And for what?

The most powerful emotion, however, was guilt.

I felt so guilty for doing this to the children. They didn't deserve it. But I also knew that the situation would only have been worse if we hadn't separated. They didn't deserve to live in such a bad atmosphere, either. It was hard.

I had the support of friends and family around me. My mother thought I should give it another try. 'For the children's sake.' I knew this was impossible. Things had gone too far. Some friends offered other pieces of advice. It was well-meaning and, in most cases, absolutely true. Yet like so many people who go through a divorce, I found it impossible to believe things like 'time is the great healer' and 'the pain will ease'. I kept thinking to myself, 'You don't understand,' even though some of them did. The most valuable friends were those who were there just to listen and lend a shoulder to cry on. There were Chris and Keith Banks, a couple to whose daughter, Nikki, I was a godmother. Keith drove a delivery van and used to pop in unannounced just to check up on me. But the most notable source of strength was Jane Simpson, who'd become my closest confidante and ally over the last few years.

Jane lived nearby with her husband, Graham. I'd met her through her sister Ruth with whom I'd worked at a local knitwear factory. She was an accounts clerk at a local garage and was a direct, outspoken person and a great one for accentuating the positives – not that there were many of them in the situation as far as I was concerned. Yet she knew too when simply to be quiet. She was a godsend.

Of the allies I had at that time, however, none were more steadfast and supportive than my dogs. If it hadn't been for them, goodness knows what would have happened to me.

By this time we had a dozen dogs. Tragically Donna had died of a tumour, aged only eight, but we had bred Sandy, the daughter of our other cocker spaniel Susie. In the course of the previous year we'd also acquired another two springers Kizzie and Honey, a pointer called Sophie, and a field spaniel, Cider. In addition to Lady and Chris we also had another English springer called Emily who I had rescued from a local home where she wasn't being well cared for, and Kizzie had provided us with three new puppies. Towards the end of our marriage, Tony had objected to the number of dogs we had. On one occasion, I think I was offered the ultimatum 'it's either the dogs or me'. I won't go into the details, but suffice it to say my reply was that if the choice was between a faithful dog or an unfaithful husband then there wasn't a choice at all. 'At least they are here for me,' I think I said.

In fact the dogs had been a huge comfort to me during the disintegration of the marriage. As we grew further and further apart, they stayed close to me. I remember one night Tony was out late again. He came home to find a mattress laid out on the bedroom floor. I was sleeping with the dogs next to me.

In the days after Tony's departure, Lady and Chris became my closest allies. Lil, as I called Lady, was my shadow. Wherever I went, she was there at my side. She was always a confident, at times dominant dog. She seemed to grow stronger and more assertive somehow, challenging anyone who came near me with her body language and regularly looking up at me as if to ask, 'Are you OK?' Again, I can now see that she sensed my vulnerability, she wanted to protect me, she knew that was her duty.

So when I put the children to bed and came down at eight o'clock in the evening, she would immediately be by my side. The moment I sat down she nuzzled up against me on the sofa where she was soon joined by Chrissy. I would often drift off to sleep there with them.

During those dark, early days, sleep never came easily. There were far too many nights when I turned to alcohol just to knock me out.

It was a coping mechanism. My tolerance for alcohol is so low I only need a sniff of the wine waiter's apron to start giggling. So it didn't need much to do the job. But I did find myself emptying the small supply of spirits Tony had left behind, mainly whisky. I didn't even like the drink, but mixed with orange juice or whatever else I had available in the fridge, it did the trick.

For a brief time, I know friends and family wondered whether I was developing a drink habit. The truth of the matter was that I had no intention of replenishing the supplies when they were gone. When the drinks cabinet was finally emptied, that was that. I barely touched a drop afterwards.

Apart from anything else, I didn't have the money for alcohol.

The immediate effect of the separation was to turn the clock back twelve years. Once more I was faced with a situation where there was no money coming into the house. Once more I had to endure the nightmare of signing on for benefits and cope with the task of somehow eking out an existence for all of us on £21 a week.

Financially these were the hardest times of all. Visiting the supermarket was a humbling experience. I'd go equipped with a calculator. If I discovered I'd exceeded the limit of what I could spend I'd put things back on the shelves. The children came first, obviously. My motto quickly became they'd have everything they needed and some of the things they wanted. I'd have to make do with what was left.

This also meant that I was now faced with the awful prospect of having to break up my pack of dogs. They were a considerable drain on my meagre resources.

Emily, the dog I had rescued, needed a lot of attention, for instance. She had been badly neglected by her previous owner and had needed an operation for her ears to be removed. Josh Cooper told me I had no choice, they were so infected she couldn't shake her head.

The operation had cost £108. Fortunately the vets allowed me to pay it off monthly. But it was still an expense I could have done without.

My affection for each and every one of the dogs was great. But the harsh fact was I couldn't keep them all. I had to decide which ones to part with.

My protectors, Lady and Chrissy, obviously had to stay. So too did the children's dogs, Susie and Sandy. In the aftermath of the separation, I wasn't there for them in the way I'd been in the past. I did my best, but they had increasingly drawn on each other. They asked to sleep in the same room. I realized they needed each other. So I bought them bunk beds. I bought them a £6 television. They had their own little world up there. The dogs were an intrinsic part of that world. They could talk to their dogs, they were their living, breathing friends. Ellie in particular drew a lot of strength from her spaniel, Susie. The two of them slept together.

In the end I decided to reduce my pack by half, keeping six and parting company with the other six. So the choice was down to six from the eight other dogs.

It was not something I undertook lightly. I put a lot of effort into finding the right homes for each of them, matching every dog with an owner that suited it.

Jane offered to buy Amy, one of my young springers, from me. I knew she'd be an ideal owner, but refused to take any money from her after all she had done for me. But she was as stubborn as me; she then refused to take Amy. In the end I offered her a compromise. I would accept money. I asked her to open her purse – and I took out ten pence. She laughed and said: 'OK, you win.' By the time all the dogs had gone to their new homes I felt a mixture of emotions once more. I was relieved that they'd all gone to good homes. I knew they'd have happy, contented lives. But my happiness was tinged with sadness. Inside I still felt as if the life I had built was slowly falling apart. The dream I'd cherished had been broken.

Chapter 14

Rock Bottom

When our doctor turned up on the doorstep one morning, a few weeks after the separation, I must have been the only one surprised to see him.

By now I wasn't sleeping and I wasn't eating. I had lost two stone. I was going downhill at a rate of knots. I can't actually remember how it happened, such was the zombied state I was in. My head was full of confusion, guilt, loneliness, anger – all sorts of feelings, none of them good. If I am honest with myself, I had almost lost the will to live. The thought of suicide flashed across my mind on more than one occasion. Fortunately, my friends and family had sensed I was becoming a danger to myself and the children.

It was agreed with the doctor that I should be admitted to the cottage hospital nearby. I was given a bed in a small room on my own. My mother and father moved into the house to look after the children. I was told to concentrate on regaining my strength. Everything else would be looked after. I was to think about myself for a brief time.

I stayed there for three days. I think I slept for the first day. There was no choice, such was the strength of the medication they gave me. When I came round the following day I felt as if I'd been sleeping for a month. By that afternoon I was sitting up in bed. Someone brought in a small black and white television. For most of the evening I just sat there staring at the screen, barely taking anything in. It was only when a concert by Barry Manilow came on that I paid it any real attention.

No matter what people may think of him as a performer, there is no question Barry has written some powerful songs. I was – and am – a huge fan. As I lay there in bed that evening, every song he sang seemed to press a button inside me. Suddenly I began screaming. All the emotions that had been bottled up inside me were released. I just let go.

The nurse appeared at the door, then shouted for the doctor. She'd been alarmed but he was as calm as could be. He came and sat with me for a while. He clearly understood that this was the best possible thing for me to do. Eventually the sobbing subsided. Of course I had no sense of it at the time, but in retrospect I can see that at that moment I had hit rock bottom. I had released all the pent-up anger and emotion inside me. The climb back up was going to be a long, slow one, but at least it could now begin. I'd made it through the rain, as Barry Manilow might have put it. The following evening I said I was ready to go home and see the children.

I remember I arrived home on a Thursday. The following morning, I got up, saw Tony and Ellie off to school and immediately got myself going. I felt I had turned a corner, it was almost as if I had a new lease of life.

The hallway had needed decorating for years. There were scuff marks and scratches around the doorways. It was gloomy and painted a depressing dark green. I hated it. I'd lost count of the number of times I'd asked Tony to redecorate it. Somehow I'd never found the time to do it myself either. I'd asked Jane to give me a hand redecorating over the coming weekend. But that morning I decided to make a start. I cleared the furniture out, put on my overalls and got stuck in.

Jane popped round late in the afternoon, to check what time I needed her the following morning. Her jaw dropped when she came in through the front door. I'd bought some brilliant white paint and started decorating by myself. The hall was now transformed. The white paint was glowing, as if the sun had been allowed into the hallway for the first time. The effect on me was just as powerful. I hadn't felt so good about something for a long time.

As the months wore on, my dogs again played their role in my rehabilitation.

Financially I knew it was going to be a tall order, but I was getting desperate to gain a toehold in the show world once more. There were all sorts of reasons for this. Apart from anything else, I needed to get back into the wider world. My early experiences of showing had been huge fun. I really enjoyed the social element of it. Dogs – and dog people – seemed more than ever like an escape from the crushing grind of home life.

It was winter and with the coastal resorts closed until the following season there were no jobs going anywhere. I was still on social security and had hardly anything spare. For a long time now I had been in the habit of putting little stashes of money – sometimes piles of coppers – in jars dotted around the house. Most of them were for essentials like kids' clothes and Christmas. I decided to start another little pile – this time for dog shows.

It proved hard building it up, however. The children always took priority and even if I had enough spare money I often found I was simply unable to commit myself to dates in the canine calendar. I was feeling pretty low when Jane rang me and asked me over to discuss 'a plan' she had.

After she had taken Amy from me she had decided to breed a litter of puppies. Jane had a good job, working in accounts for a local business. She was too busy with work to tackle the job full time, so she asked me whether I'd be prepared to raise the puppies at my house if she paid for their upkeep. She would then organize their sale and keep the proceeds. She did it out of friendship. She understood the joy dogs brought into my life, yet knew too that financially I was finding it hard to hang on to my pack, let alone acquire more dogs. It was a wonderful gesture – even if it did cause me more trouble than it was worth.

One morning that autumn, I opened the door to find a stony-faced figure on my doorstep. He announced himself as an official from the Department of Health and Social Security.

'I've been asked to investigate a report that you are operating a business breeding puppies,' he declared in solemn tones.

I was taken aback. 'I do have puppies on the premises, but they're not mine,' I explained.

He gave me a dismissive look. He clearly didn't believe me.

'I'm looking after them for a friend.'

He'd probably heard a variation on this theme a hundred times before. He didn't even bother making a note of Jane's name. He explained that he had no option but to recommend my payments be suspended. 'I will have to confiscate your payments book,' he told me.

I was so stunned that I wandered into the house and found the book. By the time I reached the door, however, my reaction had changed.

'Here's your bloody book,' I said. I threw it at him and slammed the door in his face.

I couldn't believe what had happened. I was less concerned about who had reported me than angry at the injustice of it. I was doing this as a favour.

My first phone call, naturally, was to Jane. She told me to calm down and that she'd sort it out. She is a forceful individual at the best of times. It was only later that I discovered what happened.

Jane had called the local DHSS office and let rip. At first they stonewalled her with a 'We can't comment on individual cases'. Jane had been undeterred, however.

'Jan Knight is looking after my puppies for me,' she said. She really gave them what for.

About three hours after he'd left, the same DHSS officer was back on my doorstep. 'I'd like to clarify a few things,' he said, trying to redress the situation. He asked me to explain what was going on. Clearly, my account tallied with what his colleagues had been told by Jane.

I was still angry. Since my childhood I'd hated being accused of not telling the truth. 'You're calling me a liar,' I said to him.

He had clearly been given his instructions, however. He was soon handing me back my payments book.

When Jane popped round that evening I told her what had happened. She didn't say much, but I saw a knowing smile form on her face.

That night I managed to see the funny side. But in the days that followed a quiet determination came over me. I couldn't go through that sort of humiliation again. It was demeaning, soul-destroying. I had to get a job. Any job.

So I became a Jacqueline-of-all-trades. I worked as a factory cleaner in Spilsby, I worked as a secretary for three months. I did anything and everything that was offered to me. I'd passed my driving test some years earlier, you simply couldn't exist in the countryside without being able to drive. I'd been putting money aside for a car for months beforehand. I couldn't afford anything flashy, but I bought a good, solid second-hand estate from a local dealer.

I can remember the feeling of exhilaration and em-powerment I felt as I whizzed around the country lanes, juggling school runs with assorted odd jobs here, there and everywhere.

Over the years, I've got into the habit of giving my cars names. That first one set the precedent. I called her Penny – for Independence.

Chapter 15

The Three Musketeers

During the dark days that followed the separation it broke my heart that I couldn't do more for the kids. Our first Christmas alone together was particularly hard. I had no money at all. That year the only presents I could afford were a cheap calculator for Tony and an equally inexpensive wristwatch for Ellie. At least I knew we were together, and that was more important than anything. We began to see ourselves as the Three Musketeers. It was all for one and one for all. After what we'd been through, nothing was going to split us up.

The children were my rocks. Without them I'd never have pulled through.

One summer, I got a job as a traffic warden in Skegness. I didn't particularly enjoy it. Slapping parking tickets on tourists' windscreens hardly made me the most popular person in town! But it was work – and money, so I gritted it out.

The kids were brilliant; even now they were only twelve and fourteen but they'd matured into the most wonderful friends to me. I remember I came home one Sunday ready to start the dinner. Jane had been keeping an eye on them. As I walked in I smelled the familiar aroma of a joint cooking in the oven. Ellie had got dinner on the go. Of course I told them it was the best meal I'd ever had – and in many ways it wasn't far from the truth.

Ellie knew better. She asked me how she could improve on what she'd done. She wanted to know what had worked and what hadn't, to learn from her mistakes. By the third week she was cooking the dinner to perfection. We pulled together, the three of us.

It wasn't easy. Divorce doesn't conform to the soap opera model, where people separate and remain friends afterwards and it's all hunky dory. The truth is there's trauma, there's sadness, hurt and anger. You run the gamut of emotions. And it was no different for us than it was for anyone else. It took us fully three years to get over the initial pain of the upheaval. Inside, of course, there was a part of each of us that would never heal.

I found it very hard to cope with the children's problems. The worst times were when their father would say he was coming on a Sunday but didn't turn up. They'd sit by the window all day, waiting for his car to appear. When they finally gave up I'd get the backlash. My heart went out to them.

One evening after school I noticed Tony reading a piece of paper, then hurriedly screwing it up and throwing it into the wastepaper basket. 'What was that?' I asked.

'Oh, nothing,' he said. 'Just some school stuff.'

I let it go, but picked the paper up later. I saw that it

was a letter to all parents informing them of a school trip to Moscow and Leningrad the following summer. The cost, I remember vividly, was £336.

The kids were acutely aware of how hard things were for me financially. When I asked Tony why he'd thrown the paper away, he simply said: 'I know we can't afford it, Mum, don't worry.' It was as if he'd driven a stake through my heart.

Relations were far from good with his father. But I steeled myself and had a conversation with him about the trip. We both owed it to Tony to raise the money. His father agreed he would meet half the cost.

The trip had to be paid for in instalments. I scrimped and saved every penny I could find to meet each of the early payments. Naively I suppose, I'd told myself that his father would pay the later instalments. No such luck.

It was during the spring and summer, as the final payments were due, that Tony nervously broke the news to me that he just didn't have the money. Whether he did or didn't was irrelevant. I ended the conversation with him there and then. I had more important things to do.

There were two payments left. The day before the penultimate one was due I went to see a local woman. We'd met here and there about the place and she'd always complimented me on my Victorian engagement ring. I knocked on her door and nervously explained the situation to her. 'It's yours if you'd like it,' I said.

She gave me £35 for it. The money was delivered to the school secretary the following morning.

I did a similar thing the day before the final payment had to be made. This time I headed off to a pawnbroker's in Skegness. I had gathered together all the jewellery I had left in my possession. There was my wedding ring, two necklaces and two gold bracelets. In many ways the bracelets had more sentimental value than my wedding and engagement rings. One of them was the present I'd been given up in Arbroath during my time in the Wrens. It broke my heart to give it away, but I knew I'd have felt even worse if Tony hadn't been allowed to go on the school trip.

There was something humiliating about watching the pawnbroker weighing up objects that, in very different ways, had meant so much to me during my life. To me they were priceless, now he was going to put a value on them.

'Fifty pounds the lot,' he said.

I had no option. It covered the £45 I needed for the final payment – and left £5 for Tony's pocket money.

A week later I saw him off on the coach from school. Eight days after that I was back in the playground again, watching the beaming faces filing off the bus. As the other kids disembarked, most of them were full of tales about what they'd seen or comments along the lines of 'great time'. Tony just walked up to me, smiled the widest smile I've ever seen and said: 'Thanks, Mum.'

Financially they were some of the toughest times I'd faced. Yet by saving every penny that passed through the house, we got by.

By 1983 I was finally beginning to get back into the show world in a small way. I had managed to go to a few shows here and there. It had immediately reminded me of how good showing was for me. I met kindred spirits, other people to whom dogs played a hugely important role. Money was always an issue, of course. But I'd found people incredibly helpful and supportive.

There is something slightly addictive about competition. Anyone who has taken part in dog shows will tell you this. Once the bug has bitten you are hooked. I certainly was as I dipped my toe back in the water again. My first successes this time came with Honey, who shone in a number of novice classes. Long term, however, my ambition had always been to succeed in competition with a dog that I had bred myself. So it was with this in mind that I put my former dog Amy with a show-winning springer, Genghis Khan, belonging to Glenn Miller, an owner whom I'd come to know well on the show scene.

Glenn typified the kind of person I'd met in the show world. When I'd returned to showing I had been helped by the generosity of the people I met there, many of whom offered to give me lifts to shows. Glenn was one of them.

Amy's puppies were born in 1982. The moment I set eyes on them, I knew there was a special one. I named him Khan in honour of his father.

Success didn't come easily in the show world. But by 1983 Khan had blossomed into the most successful show-dog I'd yet owned. He was now eighteen months old and had grown into a magnificent creature. Not only did he look fabulous, he had a nobility and personality, an aura about him that set him apart from other dogs. I always approached competitions with low expectations, but that year I really did think he had a chance of making it to Cruft's. Sure enough, he did.

As I travelled down to London once more, I tried to put the memories of my first, disastrous Cruft's behind me. In truth the problems I'd had then had been down to my own inexperience and nervousness. Now I was much more attuned to the showring. And in Khan I knew I had an exceptional dog. As Khan went through his paces in the ring, however, images of that first catastrophic performance were soon flooding back.

The floor was made of a very smooth concrete. As Khan was going round the ring he slipped and took the most awful tumble. The judge saw me and asked if I was all right. If I hadn't been so worried about Khan, I'd probably have started thinking about the damage I'd done to our hopes of winning the competition. But I was more concerned with making sure he hadn't damaged himself in the fall. Fortunately he was fine and what's more, he was eager to carry on with the competition.

His fall had come towards the end of his run so we had a chance to regain our composure while the other competitors strutted their stuff. I sat there holding and cuddling Khan, reassuring him that everything was all right. By the time the judge came round to inspect Khan more fully, he was back to his imperious self.

At the end of the adjudication process, the judge asks all the competing dogs to stand in a row. They then point out the winner, ushering it to join them in the middle of the arena. It's a moment of high drama in the dog world, often orchestrated by the judges who can take an eternity to put the poor contestants out of their misery.

On this occasion there was no tension at all. The judge just strode out to the middle of the arena, turned towards me and the other owners standing there and pointed straight away. At Khan.

We ran out into the middle of the arena and took in the applause. It was a wonderful moment and remains the highlight of my time in the showring.

By the summer of 1984, we had lived in Firsby for almost a dozen years. Inevitably the children – and I – had grown tired of the place. What had initially appealed about it had now become a huge negative.

When Tony and Ellie were little, the place had been a paradise for them. As teenagers, they now saw it as a prison. They wanted to meet up with schoolfriends, pop out to shops or town centres. They had bikes but they were still miles away from the places they wanted to be. It was time to make our escape.

After much toing and froing, I'd bought Tony out of the property and was now free to sell it as I saw fit. I was desperate to move the children to a more urban environment. They were desperate to be able to intermingle with children of their own age, to do the normal things that teenagers do.

I was determined to start looking for a new house. But there was no way I was going to get anywhere without talking to someone about financing the move.

One day I summoned up all the confidence I could and went to see a financial advisor in Horncastle.

I sat down, looked him straight in the eye and said: 'I want to borrow nine thousand pounds.'

He didn't know anything about me or my situation. 'What have you got to offer as security?' he asked. 'And can you give me an idea of your income?'

I told him there was some equity in the house. But I was honest and said I had only a series of part-time jobs. There was nothing permanent. Seeing him blanch a little, I took the bull by the horns. I quite surprised myself with the passion I put into the little oration I gave him.

'Look, I know I don't seem like the greatest candidate for a loan but I'm telling you I'll get a job, I'll work hard, I'll pay the mortgage in full on time every month and I'll make a life here for me and my children,' I said.

The silence was excruciating. He sat there, tapping away at his calculator, avoiding eye contact with me. Eventually he raised his head and I detected the slightest of smiles.

'I've got a feeling you're going to do what you say,' he said.

'Was that a yes?' I asked, not quite sure that he'd said what I thought he'd said.

'It was,' he replied, smiling, before reining himself in. 'I can't lend you any more than nine thousand, though.'

I could have kissed him. In fact I think I might have done.

A friend had seen a house in the village of Barnetby which he thought would suit us down to the ground. I went to see it and fell for it immediately.

Barnetby was a very picturesque little village. It was a bigger place than Firsby, but then that wasn't difficult. It had a post office, a railway station, a butcher's and a chip shop. It suited us fine, as did the house, one of two semi-detached homes on the edge of town near the church and some open fields. There was plenty of room inside and outside. I could also see there would be room for kennels and a good-sized run for the dogs during the daytime.

I immediately went to the estate agent's and put in an offer. By the end of the day it was accepted, within a few weeks we were loading up the removal lorry and saying our farewells to Firsby.

It was emotional leaving behind neighbours who had turned into good friends over the years. There were a few tears shed as we loaded the last bits and pieces into our makeshift removal van and bade our farewells. In a small community like that, everyone knew each other's business so our neighbours knew of the hard times the three of us had faced during recent years in Firsby. They understood why we had to leave. Frank and Daisy Archer, our next-door neighbours, popped round the day we were leaving and gave the children a gift each. 'We're sorry to see you go, but we know you've got to go,' Daisy said, dabbing her eyes with her handkerchief.

As the children and I shut the door for the last time I turned the lock and started pushing the keys back through the letterbox. At that moment Ellie appeared at my side. She had noticed what I was doing and had probably realized some of the thoughts that were rushing through my mind.

'Mum,' she said, holding my arm as I slipped my hand through the letterbox. 'Let's leave the sadness here with the keys . . .'

Chapter 16

Newshound

A few days after moving in to the new house I picked up the phone to hear a familiar voice on the line.

'Just thought I'd call to see how you were getting on,' the financial advisor asked.

'Fine.'

'How's the job hunting going?' he went on, the nervousness in his voice unmistakable.

'Fine,' I said, unable to resist turning the tables on him by introducing a small but significant silence. 'I start a job with the *Lincolnshire Times* on Monday.'

The change of scene had provided the impetus I needed to get my life going again. Almost immediately I'd spotted an advert for a sales executive at the local newspaper in Brigg. I'd worked in advertising before, of course. But I hadn't sold space or worked on the sales side at all. I was so determined to get things off to a good start in Barnetby that I couldn't let that deter me. I bluffed my way through the interview, dropping what I thought would be impressive-sounding names from the advertising agencies I knew of in London. It did the trick.

'You can start next Monday,' the sales boss said.

Like all good local newspapers, the *Lincolnshire Times* reflected the community it served. Brigg was a sleepy market town, where no one got terribly excited about much at all. The closest thing to a political issue was the recent decision to rename North Lincolnshire as South Humberside, something the locals resented terribly. The most widely read news reports were about the price of heifers at the weekly cattle market. So the newspaper's pages were far from racy. The *Sun* or the *Daily Mirror* it was not.

The *Times* offices were in a cramped shopfront on the High Street. There was a receptionist, two other ad reps apart from me, three reporters and a staff photographer. We all reported to the paper's head office in Hull, where the executive who interviewed me was based.

As I settled into work, I found the paper's journalistic staff mirrored its personality perfectly. The first edition of the paper had been published back in the nineteenth century. At times I felt convinced the chief reporter, Ted, had been there to witness it rolling off the presses. Ted had fallen through the administrative cracks somewhere along the line. He was well into his eighties and should have been retired a long time ago. But he loved his job and the life that went with it and had absolutely no intention of telling them that it was time for him to draw his pension. He was probably going to die at his desk or sitting in the press bench at the local magistrates' or parish council – and that's the way he wanted it.

The other main reporter, Nora, was slightly younger, probably in her fifties. But she too seemed like part of the furniture, or at least she did when you could see her. Nora was a chain smoker and walked around in a Benson & Hedges flavoured fug, coughing and spluttering all the time. Trails of fag ash followed her wherever she went.

The elder statesman and stateswoman of the paper they may have been but they were the sharpest customers in the office. There was little that got by Ted and Nora. They knew everybody and everything about the place. I used to love listening to Ted's stories about the weird and wonderful things he'd covered over the years. The offices were in a creaky old three-storey building. According to Ted, the top floor was inhabited by a female ghost. His version of who she was varied. Sometimes she was a wanton woman who had perished at the hands of her cuckolded husband, at other times she was the innocent victim of a notorious local axeman. It depended on how good a lunch he'd had at his favourite local watering hole.

Ted and Nora were such natural reporters that when there wasn't much news, they generated it themselves. I remember Nora covering the BBC's *Antiques Roadshow* when it came to the area. She arrived in the office that morning clutching a vase which she'd obviously been using as an ashtray at home. It could have contained the remains of her entire family, there was so much grey powder silted in there. But there was something intriguing about it. It was made of blue and white pottery and looked suspiciously as if it was Victorian or even earlier. She cleaned it up and took it off with her.

She came back with a broad grin on her face. She'd been told her ashtray was worth five and a half thousand pounds. There hadn't been any news to match it at the roadshow. So that week Nora became the town's big news story.

I'd had some less than pleasant experiences working in offices before. Far too often I had got into confrontations with people, particularly those in authority. I recall working as a secretary to the boss of a large knitwear factory. Part of my job was to make up the wages each Friday. Once one of the factory floor workers arrived up in the office claiming his pay packet was £30 short. I checked it and found he was right. So I made it up out of petty cash. But when the boss saw what I was doing he was not best pleased. 'Why are you wasting your time on them out there?' he said. I replied that without 'them out there' he wouldn't have a business. He told me I was skating on thin ice and should change my attitude. I didn't. I changed my job instead.

The moment I walked into the *Lincolnshire Times'* cramped offices, however, I realized this was a different place altogether. Here the atmosphere was wonderful. We all got along. I quickly felt at home.

Despite all this, however, a cloud hung over the paper. The circulation was dwindling and – as I'd quickly discovered – winkling money out of local advertisers was hard work.

I was pretty good at selling advertising. I was honest, I never tried to sell people things they didn't want. That didn't always go down well with the powers-that-be. But it got me results and a salary that included commission on what I sold. And with two children and half a dozen dogs to support, that was what mattered.

With the paper struggling so badly, any ideas for livening up the pages – and bringing in more advertising – were welcome. We were having a meeting one day when I summoned the courage to make a suggestion.

'How about a pets and animals page?'

Everyone nodded encouragingly. It would be a good source of extra advertising and would appeal to a community in which animals were an important part of life. Then after an awkward silence someone raised the only problem. 'We'd need some editorial stories to go with the adverts. Who's going to write it?'

Ted and Nora didn't take kindly to being told what to do by sales people. Someone popped into their office to ask their opinion. 'Don't know much about animals,' Ted apparently said without even raising his eyes from his typewriter. Nora muttered something similar.

'Why don't you do it, Jan?' someone said back at the meeting.

I won't deny I was excited by the idea. So I spoke to head office that afternoon. They gave it the go-ahead – provided I could sell the space around the articles.

I immediately got cracking, calling every local pet shop, kennel and cattery in an attempt to cajole them into advertising. It was as I looked through the list of potential advertisers that I came across the name that would provide me with my greatest source of stories – and much more besides.

Set in twenty acres of open country about six miles outside the town of Winterton, the JG Sanctuary was the area's equivalent of the Battersea Dogs' Home. It had been set up by a local businessman, Jerry Green, in the 1960s.

Jerry Green was a benevolent businessman with a soft spot for four-legged creatures of all kinds. Over the years he had provided a haven for dogs, cats and donkeys. He had even taken in a retired racehorse called Nev, who was still there when I visited.

Green had died in the 1970s and the sanctuary was now in the hands of his niece, Peggy Dornam. Peggy ran the sanctuary with a small staff, led by her right-hand man, Dave.

As people the two were chalk and cheese. She was the daughter of a senior RAF officer and ran the place with military precision. Always impeccably turned out, she spoke in a cut-glass accent and expected her staff to call her Miss Dornam. He, on the other hand, was a real rough diamond, born and bred in Lincolnshire and the owner of a vocabulary so colourful it would have made a Grimsby trawlerman blush. On the occasions when he wasn't swearing orders at the kennel maids, he was offering eccentric pearls of philosophical wisdom. 'Every dog deserves a fireplace,' was one of his favourites.

I don't know whether he felt he deserved the right to do so or was just being awkward, but when I arrived he was the only person who regularly referred to his boss as Miss D.

As odd a couple as they were, however, I immediately saw that Dave and Miss D. were bound by their love of dogs and united in their mission to bring a little happiness to the discarded and abused creatures that found their way into their kennels.

I spent a couple of hours there with the staff photographer then went back to the office, where I was faced with the daunting prospect of transforming my pages of notebook scribble into a coherent article.

It took me an age. Apart from anything else, I was very conscious of sitting there at the typewriter, pretending to be what I wasn't. I was petrified of Ted or Nora coming in and looking over my shoulder. I drafted, redrafted and redrafted again. My wastebasket looked like a miniature Himalaya by the time I'd finished. But I got the piece done.

The following week I picked up the paper and proudly looked at my first piece of published work. It was hardly Charles Dickens, but I felt quietly proud of myself. Midway through the morning Ted stuck his head around the corner from the editorial office. He had the paper in his hand.

'You're not a reporter, are you?' he asked.

'But you knew that?' I said, worried that he was going to invoke some union rule or custom that meant I wasn't allowed to write. My heart was pounding, I thought I'd made some terrible mistake.

'It's bloody good,' he said, smiling, waving the paper and sliding off.

Soon afterwards Nora appeared in her usual haze of smoke. She too wasn't always the most generous person with her praise. But she sidled up to me. 'Saw the piece,' she said, dragging on a cigarette. Again the pause was long enough to set my nerves on end. 'Not half bad,' she nodded. 'Not half bad. What have you got for next week?'

The great thing about that piece was that it stimulated a response. Almost immediately people were walking in off the streets and telling me all manner of tales. Among the stories I shared with my readers in the coming weeks was that of the cunning cat that had made itself four different homes in a local village. (Each house was occupied by an elderly person living on his or her own. The cat had cleverly persuaded all four of them that it regarded them as its sole owner. Four substantial daily meals were guaranteed as a result.)

I like to think I did a bit of good too. I remember I ran a successful campaign to allow an elderly lady to take her beloved cat into the residential home which she had just entered. On another occasion I found a young boy a rabbit. To be honest, it gave me far more pride than my main job. Sales was OK, but this was more exciting. I was a newshound now.

From the very beginning, it was obvious that I was going to spend a lot of time at the JG Sanctuary. Even before I'd finished my first interview with Miss D. for the paper, I'd volunteered to help out on her annual open day.

I'd had to turn down her first offer.

'Do you read fortunes, my dear? We always have a "Gypsy Rose Lee",' she'd asked me.

'I'm afraid not, Miss D.,' I replied. 'But I could run a dog show for you.'

'Smashing,' she said. 'Let me know what you need.'

Before I knew it I was organizing a show to be held that summer. It was a big success. We put on a gundog display and ran lots of novelty classes to find the dog with the waggiest tail and the most appealing eyes. I was really pleased because the previous record had been set when Miss D. had persuaded James Herriot, aka Alf White, to visit the show. That year she had raised just over £1,000. When they added up the proceeds this year we had collected £1,700.

In the wake of the show I began to get more and more involved with the place.

By this time I had eight dogs. Chrissy, Susie, Sandy, Lady, Emily and Khan had been joined by Gemma, another English springer spaniel, and a lovely beagle called Kim. Kim had been given to me by a friend. She hadn't fitted into their household and she'd asked me if I would like to give her a home. I had always wanted a beagle, so I said yes.

To some people my having all these dogs seemed odd. They'd ask me: 'Why so many?' My answer then remains the same as it is today. I look at it this way. I don't smoke, I don't drink, I don't go out much; this was – and is – my greatest source of enjoyment and recreation. I could just about afford to keep them, so that's what I did.

If I'd felt it was bad for this many dogs to be in one place I would never have kept them there. The fact of the matter was that they were thriving in the environment of the new house. There was plenty of room for them to run free. They remained by day in the large runs I'd built, then went out for long walks with me and the kids in the fields before and after work.

I felt blessed to have such great friends. Working at the sanctuary made me appreciate how lucky my dogs were to live in a happy, loving environment. The dogs at the sanctuary were nervous, often aggressive because of the hideous treatment they'd been subjected to by their owners. The sight of so many dogs starved of that affection – through no fault of their own – made me want to give something back. I didn't really have much spare time. But I gave what I had to helping out.

To begin with I spent a week mucking out the kennels and generally lending a hand. After that, Miss D. began to call me in to help with the grooming of some of its residents.

I recall a pair of dogs we called Snitter and Woof after the characters in Richard Adams's *The Plague Dogs*. They had been found in a terrible condition roaming the fields nearby. Snitter's coat was so matted it was as if she had been wrapped in a sticky bandage of hair. Woof's was in such an appalling state that great clumps of it would come off in my hand every time I touched her.

It took me many long hours of patient, hard work to reach a point where these dogs could even bear to have a brush within a yard of them. As I spent an increasing amount of my time there, I began realizing the selfless work these people were doing – for little financial reward, I might add.

Ted and the rest of the staff at the paper loved the tales I brought back from the sanctuary. Many of my articles for the newspaper revolved around them finding new homes for these canine waifs and strays. Such tales fitted in with Ted's philosophy of the perfect newspaper yarn. 'Make them smile, make them cry and make them think,' he used to say. Within the wire-meshed fences of the JB Sanctuary, there were stories that could provoke all three of those emotions at the same time.

At first I didn't really appreciate the amount of care and compassion and sheer hard work that went into running a sanctuary like this. But it didn't take me long to see things in a new light.

I was no psychologist, but I quickly came to understand

why Miss D. had decided to devote most of her life to animals. As a young woman she'd been engaged to an officer in the RAF. They were making plans for their wedding when he was killed flying one of the last missions of World War II. It took her many years to recover from the loss – and in some ways she never did.

She remained single, seemingly unhappy with life. It was only when her uncle opened his first sanctuary that she finally began to see a mission for herself. She had dedicated herself to that cause ever since. By the time I got to know her, the sanctuary provided shelter for 120 dogs at a time. Two other sanctuaries, one in Norfolk, the other in Yorkshire, had been opened in addition. Her ambition was to open a series of sanctuaries around the country. 'It would be nice to think they weren't needed,' she said to me early on in our friendship. 'But they are.'

There was something inspiring about her. Beneath the prim, stiff-upper-lipped exterior lay a heart of pure gold.

One day I was walking the land away from the main buildings and kennels and passed the cottage where the head maid, Ruth, lived. Like Dave and the seven kennel girls, she had been given the accommodation rent free as part of her job.

I noticed her outside with two dogs, a greyhound, Dudley, and a cocker spaniel, Luke.

Any enterprise of that size must have rules. And given her military heritage, Miss D. was a particular stickler for regulations. Woe betide anyone caught feeding dogs between meal times or mistreating an animal in any way. Miss D. may have been polite but she did not mince her words when she was unhappy. She was a real case of a steel fist in a velvet glove. I knew that one cast-iron rule was that the staff were allowed to have only one dog each.

Ruth told me herself that she'd had Luke for several years. I was puzzled as to how she had been allowed to have Dudley as well. She seemed reluctant to talk about it so I didn't press the matter. I didn't want to rock the boat.

And then while I was inside Miss D.'s office one day, I happened to notice a photograph of a pathetic, horribly emaciated greyhound. It was only when I looked closer that I saw it was Dudley.

I plucked up the courage to ask Miss D. about this. She told me how he had arrived having been horribly abused. 'At first we didn't think he would see out the month,' she said.

It was Ruth who saved his life.

'I've never seen anyone put so much love into caring for something,' Miss D. said quietly, her eyes fixed on the photograph. 'She fed him with a bottle, sat up all night when it was touch and go, gave him injections, pills and potions.'

As Dudley's condition had improved, he had come to spend more and more time with Ruth. At some point he had settled in her home. And there he had remained.

Rather than create a situation, Miss D. had decided to turn a blind eye. She had never told Ruth she could keep Dudley. But neither had she told her that she had to let him go.

'What are rules for if not for bending occasionally?' Miss D. told me with the arch of an eyebrow.

Of all the staff, the one person who seemed to regard his job as simply that – a job – was Dave. He was a likeable chap, but as blunt and direct a character as you could wish to meet. How badly I misjudged him too. The truth was revealed to me one day, when I saw a woman arriving with a dog that had just died. I know from painful personal experience how distressing a time that can be. It was Dave who dealt with her. But it was not a Dave that I had ever seen before.

I saw this big, gruff lunk of a man pick the dog up with all the care he would have shown if he had been holding a newborn baby. The tenderness and respect he showed was a huge support to the woman. She would have been in a terrible state about what had happened. Dave made sure she knew she had brought her dead dog to the right place.

'Don't you worry, Madam,' he soothed her. 'I'll look after her. Don't you worry.' The woman left looking as if an enormous burden had been lifted off her shoulders.

The more time I spent there, the more I felt as if I had found a home from home. And the more time I spent there, the more I began to question a world in which dogs could be driven into sanctuaries like this. What was wrong with us? Why couldn't man and his best friend live together in a more peaceful way?

Chapter 17

Educating Janice

By the spring of 1985, the writing was on the wall for the *Lincolnshire Times*.

Working in the advertising department meant I was at the sharp end. I knew the sales targets the paper needed to remain in business. It simply wasn't making them. Persuading people to part with their money had never been easy but it was becoming even harder. In the office and across the road in the pub that was many people's second home the rumours were rife. The paper was going broke. Its days were numbered.

By now we had moved to Brigg itself. I had sold the house in Barnetby and bought a nice three-bedroomed, semi-detached house near the town's main park. With another mortgage to meet and the family to feed I knew I needed to line up another job. Finding something as enjoyable as the *Times* proved a problem.

I had come across other people in the newspaper business in the area. I applied for – and got – a post with a sister paper, the *Grimsby Target*. It was a free newspaper, part of the *Grimsby Telegraph* group, and was advertising based.

I didn't stay there long. I continued to come up with ideas for features but found members of the editorial team poaching them then passing them off as their own. After a few months I'd joined the classified ads department of the *Hull Daily Mail*. Anyone who's worked on a newspaper knows the classified department is a real sweatshop. You are on the phone for eight hours a day 'cold calling' potential advertisers or taking down the details from people who are selling their sofas and fridges. You feel like a battery chicken. It was one of the unhappiest experiences of my working life.

To add to my woes, the travelling involved meant my financial situation was grim and getting grimmer. The biggest drain on my resources was the latest car. A Vauxhall Chevette, it had been rechristened the Shovit, it had broken down so often. During the eighteen months I'd had it the car had spent most of the time in the garage. By now I simply couldn't afford to spend the money needed to make it roadworthy again. I was having to get lifts or take public transport to get to work. Making it to work on time, then getting home in time for the kids was a nightmare.

After the good start we'd made in Barnetby, things had slipped again. I kept going. I didn't intend to let the children down. But the rollercoaster insecurity of it all was wearing me down, draining the spirit out of me. I was heading nowhere. We were sitting down having a chat one evening when the children sprang the surprise that was their solution.

I'd been ragging them about the importance of getting to university. Both were on track but like all youngsters needed a little push every now and again. They were getting ready for their A levels and GCSEs. That evening I'd been carrying on again about the importance of further education.

'If it's so important why don't you do it?' one of them said.

'Don't be so silly,' I replied.

'Why not? Put your money where your mouth is,' they said.

I cleared the dinner plates away that evening, thinking 'They're right, why not?' That night I lay awake for hours.

One of the things I kept telling the children was that education meant freedom. It meant they would have a choice about what they wanted to do with their lives. As I lay there ruminating I realized, of course, that was something I hadn't been given myself. The path I was supposed to take had been preordained early on. I wasn't supposed to have an education. I wasn't going to need one to be a wife and a mother. All I needed was my cookery course. The kids got me thinking. I saw that my options would change if I did a degree. I'd seen it within my own family. Again, as had been preordained, my cousin Les had gone on to become a doctor of physics and chemistry. That night I began to think I might be able to carve out a career. I thought I might be able to become a teacher, or a social worker. I was sick of doing all the rotten jobs I'd been doing, that was for sure.

I was mildly confident that I could meet the academic challenge of a degree. I felt there was more in me, that I had abilities that hadn't been tapped into as yet. I went to sleep determined to give it a go.

The mood didn't last long. By the following morning I

had begun talking myself down. 'All you've ever got is a City & Guilds "150" in catering. Why on earth would a college take you on?' I told myself. That evening, however, the kids were back on my case. They hadn't forgotten the previous night's conversation and weren't going to let me forget either.

Over the following days I mentioned it to some of the friends I'd made in the area. They were all encouraging. 'Go for it,' was the consensus. There was only one doubting voice, of course. 'Well if you fail, at least you've tried,' my mother said when I told her my plans.

Soon I'd picked up an application form for a degree in combined studies at the Grimsby College of Further Education, later to be part of Humberside University.

The form required a written answer to a question. The question was a general one, to do with society, and the reasons why some people had problems integrating into it. I gave the matter some thought, then sat down one weekend and wrote an essay. I was quite pleased with it when I'd finished, I'll admit. But I popped it in the post fully expecting that to be the last of the matter.

To my surprise a letter arrived soon afterwards inviting me for an interview. I've since got to know one of the members of the panel I met that day. Pete Adamson and I worked together some time later on Radio Humberside. Back then, however, we were strangers to each other.

He told me that he'd liked the essay. 'There's only one problem,' he said. 'There's no bib.'

I had no idea what he was talking about. And my bafflement must have been written all over my face.

'There's no bibliography,' he explained sympathetically.

165

'Obviously you've drawn your arguments from other sources. It's standard practice to list them at the bottom of the essay.'

'Sorry, I thought you wanted my ideas. They're all my own,' I said, feeling a bit of a twit.

I hadn't really shaken off my sense of embarrassment when Pete and the rest of the panel told me I could go. They said they'd write to me in confirmation. They said something about the place being unconditional, but I didn't really take it in. To be honest, I was glad to get out of there.

When I got home I immediately rang a friend, Pat.

'What exactly did they say to you?' she asked.

'Well they said my place was unconditional, or something like that,' I replied. 'What does that mean?'

'You silly bugger,' she laughed down the phone. 'It means you're in. They've offered you an unconditional place, they've accepted you.'

The modern, grey, concrete walls of Grimsby College of Further Education weren't exactly the dreaming spires of an ancient university. I wasn't a hairdresser either, unless you count trimming dogs' coats, I suppose. I certainly can't remember having a lecturer that looked like Michael Caine. But, in one fundamental aspect, my three years at college could have come straight off the pages of Willy Russell's *Educating Rita*, one of the most popular films of the 1980s. Just as it did for Julie Walters' character, the experience changed my life completely.

I had had my doubts about becoming a student at the

age of thirty-nine. I'd had chilling visions of sharing a classroom with dozens of people of Tony's age.

To my relief, I wasn't the only 'mature' student on the course. In fact, I was far from the oldest member of the class. There was an ex-miner and an ex-policeman looking to re-educate themselves. And there was a woman of fifty-three who was determined to get her degree as a stepping stone to a career in teaching. It was a lovely, lively blend of people. The combined studies course, as the name suggests, blended several disciplines. During my three years there I studied sociology, history and literature. I couldn't get enough of it. It was liberating, empowering – life-changing stuff.

I read more than I've ever read in my life. I'd lie there on the sofa into the small hours. It brought me and the children closer than ever too.

I remember my mother coming round one evening to discover Tony, Ellie and me all poring over our books. Tony's A levels were imminent, as were Ellie's GCSEs. Her response, of course, was typical. She couldn't resist running a finger through a film of dust she'd detected on a shelf. 'Look at the dust here, Janice,' she tutted, breaking the library-like silence. 'All that time with your head in books. You're letting the place go.'

The three of us just looked quietly at each other and smiled. On another occasion, in the summer, Tony, Ellie and I were talking about Beckett's *Waiting for Godot*. By a strange coincidence we were all studying it. 'What the hell are you lot on about?' a voice suddenly asked.

We all looked round to see our neighbour, peering over the top of the fence. 'Are you all on drugs or something?'

Of all the subjects we did, it was psychology and behaviourism that fascinated me the most. I was particularly interested in B.F. Skinner and his ideas on behaviourism, the notion that people can be programmed into acting in certain ways. It was a powerful moment for me. As I started to think about my life, I could see that I had been playing the roles that other people had imposed on me: dutiful daughter, wife, mother. I'd been conditioned to go along with it, to conform. It had brought me great joy in the shape of the children. But I did begin to wonder how things might have been different if I'd been armed with that sort of information earlier in my life.

Yet despite this I never truly felt I belonged at college, if I'm honest. I was always haunted by the idea that I wasn't good enough, that everyone else was brighter and better than me. The tutors were hugely supportive of me. And I constantly surprised myself with the course work I was doing. I was getting B pluses and sometimes better. After two years I passed the DHE, Diploma of Higher Education, which allowed me to go to the university's college in Hull to complete the final, degree year. For me none of it would mean anything until I got through the final exams and had some letters after my name.

The pressures piling up on me didn't make things any easier.

The job of juggling my studies with keeping the house going was never easy. I was getting a student grant but it wasn't enough to raise the children. So I took on a variety of jobs. I worked in the local pub in Barnetby three or four nights a week. And I even put my City & Guilds catering skills to good use, working at an old people's home in Wrawby a few miles away. My mother would have been proud of the way I turned out enough roast beef, mashed potatoes, apple pie and steamed pudding to feed a small army twice a week.

The kids, as ever, were a great help too. Both were old enough to get part-time jobs of their own. Ellie assisted in the kitchens of the pub. Tony made himself a few extra pennies helping out at the workshop of a local pine stripper. Between us we earned enough money to put food on the table and pay the bills. It was, in many ways, one of the happiest times we'd had.

The pressures of studying got to us all at times, particularly when we were coming up to exams. You could feel the tension in the house some nights. Every now and again I'd call a time-out and we'd do something silly like have a picnic in the middle of the living room. We helped each other out.

For me animals provided the other great escape. Time to show my dogs was obviously at a premium – as was the money to get around the country. But I remained as involved as possible in the local dog community.

In the meantime, horses had become an increasingly important part of my life. The sheer pleasure I took from being out and about on horseback was immense. Through the children I had become friendly with a well-known local horsewoman, Wendy Broughton, who let me ride China, a former racehorse, at her home near Brigg.

Riding along I felt the pressures of college and looking after the home lift off my shoulders. It was a wonderful release. I felt as free as a bird.

I sat my finals in the early summer of 1990, working as

hard as I had at any time in my life. And when it came to the exams, I found each of the papers reasonably straight-forward. Like every student that's ever sat an exam, how-ever, no matter how much my head told me I'd done well, the doubts still clung. I'd lie in bed at night mulling over the permutations. By the time it came to the day the degrees were announced I was paralysed with fear.

The phone began to ring early in the morning. Friends I'd made on the course were calling to ask if I wanted a lift into Hull, where the results were pinned unceremoni-ously to a wall at the university building.

I couldn't face it. It was left to a friend, Catherine, to call me.

'You've got a 2.2, the same as me,' she said. 'You've passed.'

I just sat at the kitchen table in silence. It didn't matter if I never put the degree to any use whatsoever. The important thing was that I'd proven to myself that I could do it. For the first time since my marriage break-up, I regretted the fact that there wasn't a drop of alcohol in the house. I made up for it later that night though.

Tony was in France, studying in Lyon as part of his own university course at Kingston-upon-Thames, on the day of the degree ceremony but Ellie came along. Within a year or so she too would be on her way to university, in her case Swansea, where she was to embark on a career in teaching. I invited my mother and father too. My mother's only comment on seeing the hordes of people decked out in their gowns and mortar boards was just what I'd have expected again: 'Don't a lot of people get these degrees.' But she wasn't going to take the shine off the day.

For a while I considered going into teaching myself. But the more I looked into it, the less enamoured I was of the entire system and the way it turns out robots rather than teachers.

I didn't want to be a robot – I felt like I'd been one for half my life already. This was the doorway to something new. I didn't know what – but I looked forward to finding out.

Chapter 18

Breaking Through

Armed with a degree, I decided to look for a job. I felt sure I could find something a bit more fulfilling than cleaning factory floors, rustling up roast dinners or pouring pints. I had always enjoyed caring for people. It was why I'd welcomed foster children to Firsby during the early years of my marriage and worked for voluntary groups like the St John's Ambulance. I set my sights on something that combined this with the knowledge I'd gained studying for my degree.

I had little trouble getting a job with the local social services department. I was hired as a 'programme worker' at the Brigg Resource Centre, a day centre for people with learning disabilities.

On the surface, my job title sounded rather cold and impersonal, a little like a systems analyst or a computer operative. In fact it was the opposite. My role was to work closely with a group of 'clients' (in my case nine), people with learning disabilities. I had to work with them at the centre and in their home and liaise with their families.

The group I was allocated had a wide range of disabilities.

There were people with Down's syndrome, others with cerebral palsy. Some could communicate well with the world. Others were lost to it completely.

It was challenging work, of that there was no doubt. But it gave me enormous satisfaction. It felt useful, important even. As far as I was concerned my job was about breaking through, about communicating with each and every one of my clients. It didn't always happen, far from it. But the breakthroughs I did achieve made the hardship worthwhile.

Two particular cases spring to mind – for differing reasons.

Caroline was one of the most severely disabled clients at the centre. In the time she'd been visiting, she hadn't made any progress. She was locked into her own world. She didn't communicate in any way.

I was interested in trying different approaches that might stimulate the clients. I'd read somewhere about how powerful smells had produced significant reactions in some severely handicapped people. So I introduced aromatherapy sessions at the centre. I rubbed various oils – lavender, jasmine, musk – into the clients' hands. From the comments I got back from them, I saw that it was popular.

The one aspect of the job I had already taken a dislike to was its bureaucracy. Far too often, I found myself and the other carers being given directives by faceless figures from somewhere within the social services department. It was very frustrating. Three months after I'd introduced the aromatherapy sessions, one of these bureaucrats suggested I give it up.

'It's having a negligible effect,' he said.

I begged to differ, of course. As usual, I passionately

argued my corner. And on this occasion, at least, I prevailed.

'But we will review it again in six months or so,' the executive said.

One day about a month later I was preparing to start a little aromatherapy session. I had brought the bottles out and had taken the top off one of them. Caroline, the only client who hadn't responded at all to this – or indeed to anything else we'd tried – was sitting in her usual chair, a few yards from me. Suddenly and slowly she extended her arms out in front of her. She knew what was coming and was looking forward to it. It may not sound much, but within the context of her terribly restricted life, this was a major breakthrough. I was quite emotional about it afterwards. When I told her mother this she was very excited too.

A few weeks later she told me that it had led to another significant development at home. Whenever Caroline's father arrived in the living room and spoke, she would now extend her hands in the same way – as if to greet him. To them this was the most profound piece of communication they had ever seen from Caroline. They had nothing but praise for the work the centre had done in helping them.

My happiness was, I must admit, tinged with resentment at the way the red tape within the social services hierarchy had done their best to make sure this would never happen. If I'd expected Caroline to act as proof of the need for patience and persistence, as well as a little imagination, however, I was soon sorely disappointed.

One of the most difficult clients we had at the Brigg centre was a young woman called Maggie. Like Caroline, she couldn't communicate. In her case, however, it was clear that this was a source of terrible frustration and, at times, rage. When she failed to make herself understood, she could become extremely aggressive and violent. She would turn most of the aggression on herself, ripping off her clothes or making the only noise she could, a loud shout.

It was terrible to behold. She was so desperate to communicate with people.

I had studied and read about some of the imaginative treatments that psychologists and therapists had originated in recent years. This time, however, I came up with something of my own. I started using a picture book to help her express herself more clearly.

Over a period of about three months, I put together an album of photographs. In it I placed every element of Maggie's life – pictures of each of her carers, each of the rooms in the centre, the places in the town that she visited. When she wanted to communicate Maggie would pick up the book and point to the appropriate pictures. If she wanted to do some painting, have something to eat, or even go to the toilet, she could point at a photograph or an image that explained this. It was hardly rocket science, but, again, within the context of the work we were doing, it felt like a big breakthrough.

For a while, Maggie's behaviour improved enormously. There were still occasional outbursts of anger. But in general she was able to make herself understood. It was a measure of the importance of the book that Maggie walked around cradling it throughout her time at the centre.

But then one day I arrived to discover Maggie distraught

and lashing out at everyone around her. It didn't take long to work out what had happened. She'd misplaced her book. I reassured her that we'd find it and set off to talk to the other staff members.

I could hardly believe the reaction. 'We couldn't find it,' one of them said, as if it was of no significance whatsoever. 'We've looked everywhere, she's probably hidden it somewhere,' another said.

I spent the entire day scouring every nook and cranny of that building. But to no avail. Maggie's book was her voice. And she'd lost it – again.

Incidents like that made me so angry. I couldn't bear the idea that other, supposedly professional people could care so little about their fellow humans. I'd come home feeling a mixture of emotions. Sometimes I'd be happy, others deeply frustrated. Thankfully, the dogs were there for me – whatever my mood.

The work I was doing at the centre was making me think deeply about communication. Inevitably it got me thinking about the way I was interacting with my dogs too.

I'd always been uneasy with the essentially violent, confrontational nature of traditional training – obedience training, as it was universally known. Even that word had connotations that made me queasy.

I'd tried to apply some of the things I'd been learning to my dogs. They were minor modifications really, for example softening the language used so as to move away from what I increasingly saw as the unnecessarily forceful and aggressive principles of traditional training. I knew they weren't going to change the world for dogs, but at least they would make my own dogs' lives a little better.

Looking back on it now, I can see that I had reached a crossroads. I was ready to take on ideas, to see things that perhaps I wouldn't have done at other times in my life. Subconsciously I was assembling a jigsaw in my mind. The final pieces of that puzzle revealed themselves all at once one day in the autumn of 1990.

I had just been riding China around the paddock at Wendy's farm. Wendy and I were having a cup of tea when she showed me a clipping from *Horse and Hound* magazine. It advertised that the American cowboy and 'horse whisperer' Monty Roberts was going to be working at the Wood Green animal sanctuary at St Ives, Cambridgeshire. He was appealing for difficult horses to be volunteered.

'I've put Roger in and she's been accepted,' Wendy said, with a raised eyebrow.

'Oh goodness, he's in for a shock,' I smiled back. Roger was our nickname for Ginger Rogers, Wendy's beautiful thoroughbred mare. Whenever I visited Wendy to ride China, I'd see Ginger Rogers running free in the paddock. She was a magnificent, chestnut-coloured horse – but with a will and a mind all of her own. She had attitude.

She was too young to be saddled and ridden yet. But with the day fast approaching when she would be, Wendy knew already that she would have the devil's work getting Roger to accept someone on her back. Wendy was a brilliant trainer, and would have prevailed in the end. But she knew this horse was a free spirit, an untameable force of nature – or so we thought.

Monty Roberts had staged a show in the area the previous year. Wendy had invited me along. She was terribly excited about seeing him, having read a lot about his ability to control even the wildest of horses using a completely natural, non-violent technique. He'd already been connected with articles on 'horse whispering', and this was before the book and the film starring Robert Redford had given that phrase a worldwide coinage.

To be honest, I was so wrapped up in my studies for my finals that I hadn't given it much thought at all. That was not to say I was sceptical about him. The only thing I knew about him was that he had been brought over here by Her Majesty the Queen. When it came to horses, as far as I was concerned there were few people in the country with the knowledge and passion of the Queen. If she had seen something in him, then he must be worth having a look at, I reasoned.

We had joined a smallish crowd of about fifty people, congregated about a strange circular pen. I was half expecting a John Wayne-style cowboy in leather chaps, spurred boots and stetson. What I saw instead was a neat, rather dapper man in a blue canvas shirt, tan slacks, with a blue cravat and a flat cap.

He went through a routine involving a horse that had apparently never been ridden before. His strange ritual lasted for about half an hour. At the end of that time, lo and behold, he had one of his assistants riding the horse beautifully around the perimeter of the pen. Wendy and I enjoyed the show. But, truth be told, we thought that's what it was – a piece of pure entertainment. We headed back home fairly convinced that we had seen a carefully choreographed act. 'They must be trained in advance,' Wendy said. And I pretty much agreed with her. It was too good to be true.

This time, however, it was a different matter.

We travelled down with the horsebox. When we arrived at the sanctuary, a member of Monty's team met us and led Roger into the familiar round pen for an assessment. Monty was there watching outside the perimeter of the pen. It was he who then asked the questions. His main concern was to establish that this horse was a complete novice when it came to being ridden.

'This horse definitely hasn't had a saddle on her back?' he asked.

'No,' Wendy replied.

'Never had a bridle on her head?'

'No.'

'Never had a bit in her mouth, never had a rider on her back?'

'No, never,' Wendy replied.

'OK, we'll use her for what we call the "baby starter",' Monty said.

Both Wendy and I were impressed by his emphasis on honesty. We were already beginning to rethink our ideas that this was some sort of fix.

That evening we sat down outside the pen and watched a minor miracle take place.

I've written before about the dramatic events I witnessed that day. While Monty was introducing himself, Ginger had appeared over his shoulder and begun nodding animatedly. It drew howls of laughter from the audience. It was as if she was gently mocking the speech Monty was giving.

When Monty spotted what was going on he simply smiled gently. He knew what was about to follow.

Wendy and I sat transfixed as Monty moved around his trademark round pen, carefully going through his routine.

I know now that if there is an element of showmanship in what he does it lies in the way he predicts what is to come. Slowly we saw him predict, then achieve, a series of breakthroughs. First he said he was going to get the horse to turn its inside ear to him. Roger started running around, but Monty used his body to make her change direction. As Roger ran around, however, we saw her tilt her head inward, towards the centre of the ring and the voice talking calmly yet authoritatively there.

Next, again as predicted, Roger slowly began moving away from the outside wall and making her circular runs tighter. She was coming slowly but inexorably towards Monty in the middle. Throughout all this Monty held Roger's eyes; he had fixed on to her and was not going to let go.

Now, as Monty had explained she would, Roger slowed down and began lowering her neck to the floor of the pen as she trotted. Soon her head seemed to be virtually bouncing along the floor.

Finally, as Monty had foretold during his talk, she began licking and chewing. This, he had said in his speech, was the signal that the horse had accepted him, that it was no longer afraid of the stranger so close to it.

It was at that magic moment that Monty took his eyes off Roger and turned his body sideways on. Roger stopped moving. And then as Monty began arcing away from her, she began to follow him. She was utterly relaxed, she wasn't sweating, she wasn't twitching, she was completely comfortable with this man. Slowly we saw him winning Ginger Rogers' trust. All this had happened within ten minutes. During that time Wendy and I hadn't said a word to each other. We'd both been completely transfixed.

With this achieved Monty moved on, bringing out a saddle and other riding equipment and placing them gently on the floor of the pen. Slowly, methodically and calmly he began putting the tack on Roger. First the saddle, then the bridle and the bit. With all this on, he signalled for a jockey to come into the ring. The rider gently eased himself on to Roger, slipped his left foot into a stirrup and placed himself on the saddle. Within moments, he was releasing Roger and walking her around the ring.

My reaction, I remember, was a mixture of disbelief and belief. I couldn't credit what I'd seen. But at the same time I was certain that what I'd witnessed was real.

To Wendy and me, at least, it was nothing less than a miracle. In the space of twenty-three and a half minutes, this remarkable man had achieved something that would have taken Wendy days, weeks, maybe even months.

Neither of us is short of a word or two to say for ourselves. We drove back in the horsebox to Lincolnshire in silence – each of us struck dumb by the wonder of what we had witnessed.

Back at Wendy's house Ginger Rogers was transformed. Before she'd met Monty, she'd had poor manners. She was the type of horse that would mug you for a Polo mint. Now she was as good as gold. She'd follow me and Wendy around like a shadow. It was hard to believe it was the same horse.

In the days that followed, Wendy and I couldn't stop talking about it. She was determined to learn his method and was already talking about erecting a round pen at her stables. My thoughts were heading in a different direction. I couldn't help wondering how the same principles could be applied to dogs. Surely something like this was possible with dogs, surely there was an unknown, invisible language through which we humans could connect and communicate with them. I assumed someone must already have done this. In the days and weeks after seeing Ginger Rogers transformed, I looked everywhere for the book or magazine article in which Monty's 'join up' method, as it was known, was adapted for canines. I couldn't find it.

I was sitting chatting with Wendy and Tony one day when I mentioned it. 'I can't believe no one has done this for dogs,' I said. Tony looked at Wendy and Wendy looked at Tony. I knew what they were going to say before they even said it.

'Why don't you do it?'

At first I thought they were being silly. But then I realized that, in many ways, I was ideally placed. I lived with and loved dogs. And, on a similar level, my working life involved finding ways of communicating. I didn't say as much to either of them. But in my mind I resolved to give it a go. Why not? What did I have to lose?

In the aftermath of my degree, I'd been through a time of inertia. I hadn't been really sure what I wanted to do. Now here was the challenge that I'd been waiting for. I started mapping in my mind the sort of studies I might be able to begin to work it out. I became a woman with a plan.

Unfortunately life, as John Lennon so memorably said, is what happens in between your plans. And life was about to deflect me from my new goal.

Chapter 19

Parting Company

Years earlier, the idea of returning to live with my parents would have been unthinkable. In September 1991, however, I had little alternative.

By now both the children were well ensconced at university, Tony at Kingston and Ellie at Swansea. I had sold the house in Brigg and was looking for somewhere else to live. In the meantime, however, both Mum and Dad had become ill. My mother was beginning to suffer from dementia. She seemed to be living in a world of her own and had started showing signs of obsessive behaviour. But it was my father who was more worrying. In the past year or so he'd become very thin. He hardly ate. By that autumn he was complaining of almost constant pain, throughout his body. He was a strong, stoic man. He had never been one to moan when he was ill. But just looking at the way his face regularly contorted, I could see he was in agony. I could also sense what was wrong with him.

When I agreed to move into their house in Scunthorpe, I said that I would only stay until I found a new place for myself. Deep down I sensed I would be there longer than I expected.

My relationship with my parents had never been easy. It was often complex and, where my mother was concerned, highly charged. Yet in recent years we had become incredibly close. I knew I had to take charge of the situation. And the first thing I did with my father was to get him to go for a proper check-up at the local hospital, the Scunthorpe General.

We went on 28 October 1991. I remember it vividly. He was put through various tests and it was eventually agreed to give him an X-ray. We sat around for what seemed like an eternity. When they brought the results back, the evidence was unmistakable. The image was white.

My dad gave me a look. He didn't say anything. He didn't need to.

The doctor started talking generally. 'We need to address the pain you are in, Mr Fennell,' he said. 'We'll keep you here in the hospital for a while and get the medication you need organized.' A wheelchair was brought in and he was driven off to the ward where a bed was already being prepared for him.

'Miss Fennell, could you come back?' the doctor said.

I knew what was coming, but it didn't make it any easier to walk back into the room.

'I'm afraid your father is riddled with cancer,' he told me. It turned out the X-rays and the other tests had revealed he had cancer of the lungs, liver, bone and bowel. 'Could he take being told?'

'He doesn't need to be told,' I said. 'He knows.'

The doctor offered to help me explain, but I was sure I had to do this myself. 'Leave it to me,' I said.

I went to the ward to find my father. He saw me coming and just looked at me.

'That's it, isn't it, duck?' he said. 'It's all over.'

I just nodded and started crying.

My dad gave me a hug. 'I'm sorry I've been such a stroppy bugger at times,' he said.

Because he was going to be kept in, I had to head home to get some clothes. We were only ten minutes away so I arrived home quickly.

I found my mother pottering around. While I had harboured my fears about Dad's condition for a long time, she seemed totally oblivious to the seriousness of the situation. Either that or she was in denial. Whatever the truth, she genuinely didn't have a clue what was coming.

I sat her down and told her what I'd been told back at the hospital. The words didn't come easily. I broke down as I did it. She sat there, stunned for a moment. Then she turned to me and said: 'What's going to happen to me?'

I left my mother there to go back to my father. On the ward I'd been told he'd be given medication immediately. He had been in agony when I left him. I expected to find him relaxed and probably sleeping. Instead he was sitting up in his bed, looking as uncomfortable and distressed as I'd ever seen him.

'Is the pain easier, Dad?' I asked.

'Not really, they haven't given me anything yet,' he grimaced.

I was so angry. I stormed over to the nurses to find out

what was happening. They gave me some limp excuses. I just shouted at them.

'He is in agony. He needs something,' I said. The faces that looked back at me were as blank as those of sheep.

'Now,' I shouted. 'He needs it now.'

Of course it was pure anger on my part. I was angry at them for not easing my father's pain, but I was also angry at life itself. It all boiled over at that moment. It achieved the desired result though. Soon afterwards a doctor turned up. But he was, if anything, less inspiring than the nurses. He began to explain what they were planning to do. They were going to keep him here for a day or two then move him on to a hospice.

'What for, so another bunch of strangers can neglect him?' I said.

I'd seen enough in the short time we'd been there to know what had to be done.

'Don't worry, I'm taking him home with me,' I told the doctor. 'He needs to be with people who care for him.'

Over the next few days, I organized nursing and treatment for him at home. We enlisted the help of the local Marie Curie nurses, who were utterly fantastic in every way. By now Dad was too weak to even climb the stairs. The Marie Curie nurses came in and helped me set up a bed for him in the living room. A district nurse began calling in twice daily to administer morphine.

His decline was rapid.

He celebrated his seventy-second birthday on 7 October. By the following week it was clear he didn't have long. The dosage of morphine was being increased steadily almost by the day to combat the pain. It was in his bones by now. I couldn't imagine the agony he was in. He was a proud man and told me he didn't want anyone visiting him when he looked so terrible and weak. He didn't want his grand-children coming to see him like this.

But we couldn't keep family away. He came from such a tight-knit clan that people arrived from London, including my cousin Maureen, who'd been in the singing group with us all those years ago. At first he was angry at me for letting her see him. But after she'd spent some time with him, laughing and joking about the old days in Fulham, he'd relented. 'Tell them it's OK to come home,' he said, referring to Tony and Ellie.

That November I organized an early Christmas. Tony and Ellie returned from university, my nephews Dave and Ronnie came up from London with their wives, Kim and Michelle. My father was too ill to leave the bed. We had a traditional turkey meal – or veggieburger for Ellie and me – then took it in turns to go in and spend some time with him. We all knew we were effectively going in to say goodbye. Tony and Ellie in their turn went to sit with him.

The strength of the morphine he was being given meant that he wasn't coherent a lot of the time. He managed to ask me to buy a final Christmas present for my mother, however. 'Get her a gold locket, she's always wanted one,' he said. He gave it to her that night. I was there to see it. 'I won't make it to Christmas, love,' he said. 'This is to remind you of how much I always loved you. You were my world, from the moment I set eyes on you.' For a few seconds they looked like the lovestruck couple that I'd spent my childhood with. For the first time in a long time, I felt like I was in the way again. Only this time I didn't resent it one bit.

The following week Tony and Ellie went back to their universities. I had dropped Tony off at the railway station on Friday night and I got back to find one of the nurses, Jackie, there. It was clear there was something wrong. Mum was behaving very oddly, wiping work surfaces down with her handkerchief and polishing her slippers with a dish-cloth. Jackie smiled at me and said: 'We haven't got long now, I think he's slipping away from us.'

I dropped off to sleep at some point that night. It had been hard, exhausting work looking after him, keeping up with my job and everything else.

At 4 a.m. the nurse who was with us that night, Debbie, roused me. 'Do you want to come and sit with him?' she said. Her meaning was clear. The time had arrived.

I asked Mum if she was coming. 'In a minute,' she said. She didn't appear downstairs, however. She pottered around in the bathroom for a while. My father's breathing was very weak by now. Slowly it grew fainter and fainter.

At 6.55 a.m. Dad died.

The sense of relief I felt was huge. He had been in a deep coma for the past few days. Now finally he was out of pain.

By 9 a.m. the undertakers had arrived to take Dad away. I remember Mum was in the kitchen making bacon and eggs for herself as he was carried out.

'They're taking him away now,' I said.

'OK,' she said.

I have no idea what was going through her mind.

She was in a terrible state at the funeral. It was obvious to me afterwards that I couldn't leave her. We spent the following months together, muddling through as best we could. Her mood swings could be terrible. She was taking massive doses of paracetamol. I didn't know it, but she was getting neighbours to buy them for her. There were times when she was good and others when she was bad. Frequently I despaired. I thought: 'This is my life now.'

In November 1992, she fell badly in the dining room, breaking her hip. She was admitted to hospital where she had an operation to repair it. The nurses there found her difficult. After a while, she was officially diagnosed as suffering from a form of dementia. Somehow, that eased the guilt I felt.

On 16 November I went in to see her. She looked very frail. Her lips were blue. 'I'm dying for a ciggie,' she said. 'You can't have one, Mum, you know that,' I said to her.

I had to pop out for a couple of hours to run errands. I told her I would be back at three o'clock. 'Everything's going to be OK, isn't it, Janice,' she said to me. I smiled and nodded.

When I got back to her room at 3 p.m. I found a 'Do Not Enter' sign on the door. A nurse saw me and pulled me gently to one side.

'We've been trying to reach you,' she said. 'It's bad news, I'm afraid. Your mother died earlier this afternoon.'

My mother's funeral took place a week later. At the same crematorium where I'd said goodbye to my father, I bade my final farewells to my mother as well.

All manner of thoughts went through my mind that day,

of course. I felt guilt at having left her that day, at leaving her to die alone.

I hated myself for some of the thoughts that went through my mind. I kept thinking, 'I'm free.'

The most consoling thought, however, was that my mum and dad were back together again. Since they first set eyes on each other in Fulham after the war, they'd been inseparable. Death had prised them apart briefly. But their love for each other was too strong for that to last for long. Mother's funeral was on the first anniversary of Father's. A year to the day after she said goodbye to him, she was saying hello again somewhere.

Losing one's parents is a traumatic experience at any time. But to lose them both in a year, and in the circumstances it happened, knocked me for six. I didn't know what to think or do. I still had my job, which was a huge consolation. But the children were away and I had no immediate family left apart from my nephews in London.

I remained in my parents' house in Scunthorpe, but started house hunting once more. As I picked up the pieces, I drew strength too from the horse I had acquired during the dark days of the last year. It had been my dad who had encouraged me to get my own horse. It was before his final decline, but he had clearly come to realize the importance of enjoying life. When I mentioned I was thinking of getting a horse he said: 'Don't wait, just do it.'

The next weekend I saw a note in the *Yorkshire Post*, advertising a horse for sale. I drove to Goldthorpe, between Barnsley and Doncaster. My budget was modest, to say the least. So I was not expecting to acquire Red Rum or Shergar. I was still shocked at what I saw.

'I'd better warn you now,' said the stables owner. 'This one is in a bit of a state.'

That was the understatement of the year. The poor creature I saw was a skeleton with flesh on its back. He was five years old and in a terrible state.

'I daren't tell you where he came from or else you'd be straight round there to sort them out,' he said, sensing my mood.

I had actually looked at two other horses. One was a magnificent bay, which had been successful in competitions as a show jumper. The moment I clapped eyes on the poor creature in Goldthorpe, however, I knew what I was going to do.

I rang Karen Rimes, a friend of mine, who was working at a livery stable. I told her about the horse's condition, but she was supportive. 'We can do it,' she said comfortingly.

Karen and I worked hard in rehabilitating Raffie, as I had named him. I would take him for short fifteen-minute walks to build up his strength. I was so paranoid, I used to cover him in a blanket in case anyone saw his skeletal body and jumped to the wrong conclusions. Slowly but surely, I undid some of the damage his previous owner had inflicted upon him.

The pleasure I got from riding was immense. But it could not relieve me of the loneliness I felt, particularly in the home that until a year previously, I had shared with my parents.

Once more I found myself turning to familiar friends. The trauma of that year had been deepened further by the loss of another of my dogs. Susie, the cocker spaniel that had meant so much to Tony and Ellie when they were younger, passed away. She lived to a ripe old age. But it was a bitter blow to lose her.

Khan, Sandy and Kim remained with me, but each of them was getting old too.

On the Sunday before Christmas that year I bought a new dog, a beautiful black German shepherd. I'd always been wary of having one. Somehow I'd felt I wouldn't be up to the challenge of looking after such a powerful, big dog. Now, however, I felt no fear. I loved the breed and wanted one. So I got one.

I didn't really approve of the woman who had bred her. She struck me as someone who didn't care about dogs, who bred them for money alone, something I utterly despise.

That night, however, I didn't care. I drove home with the puppy on my lap. I introduced her to the old gang and, so as to make her really feel at home, let her snuggle up alongside me in bed on that first, cold night.

Subconsciously, I suppose, I was reacting to the loss of my parents still. In the face of their deaths, I was reaching out for new life. Sasha, as I'd decided to call her, formed an immediate bond with me. It was the same safe, secure, unconditional affection I'd experienced all those years ago with Shane, my first dog. In the early weeks of her time with me, she slept on the floor in my bedroom. The familiar glow of friendship I felt around me helped get me through the nights.

Chapter 20

Happy Chappies

All my dogs had been unique characters. They ranged from imperious, dominant individuals like Donna to nervous, insecure creatures like poor Purdey, from strong, noble types like Khan to quiet, happy-go-lucky creatures like Kim, the beagle. From the moment Sasha arrived in my home, however, it was clear a new and very different personality had arrived on the scene. It was equally obvious she was going to revolutionize life in my pack. As it turned out, she revolutionized my life with it.

In the wake of my mum and dad's passing, Sasha brought a breath of fresh and vibrant air to what had been a rather sad and sombre household. Her youth, of course, was in stark contrast to the remaining members of the old guard. The trio of Sandy, Kim and Khan knew each other well. They had long since come to an accommodation with each other. They were used to their housemates' ways. Sasha arrived in their midst like a bombshell. She really shook the place up – and her new companions had very mixed opinions about it.

Sasha was full of youthful vim and vigour. She bounded

around the place with an incredible energy. The old guard reacted to this kinetic newcomer in their own ways. Kim, the beagle, simply ignored the young upstart. Khan, always a sociable creature, became a regular playmate. Khan had a great dignity and charisma about him. He was the kind of dog other dogs followed. Sasha latched on to this immediately. She really took to Khan and became his shadow, trailing after him wherever he went. They could have been siblings, such was the bond between them.

The real clash of personalities was between Sasha and Sandy. Sandy was a strong personality too. Her disdain for this young upstart was unmistakable. She was twelve years old, enjoying the twilight of her life and simply wasn't interested in having a child buzzing around. To begin with she simply avoided her, turning her head away whenever Sasha appeared near her. Sasha was already a physical presence, however. She was a bigger, more powerful dog and used this superiority to simply barge her way into Sandy's space. Sandy's reaction was to let out a low, grizzly growl and to curl her lip menacingly. The message was clear: 'If you know what's good for you, stay away.'

In the wake of the lows of the previous year, I had become more devoted than ever to my dogs – even when they were misbehaving and falling out with each other. They were my great release from the sometimes overwhelming troubles of the world. They were a calming influence. Sasha's arrival and the reaction it caused gave me something else, however. Watching – and sometimes defusing – these clashes got me thinking once more about the idea of canine communication and of adapting Monty Roberts' ideas. This time I made some progress.

Clearly what was going on with Sasha had something to do with status, with the issue of who was top dog within the home. I was fascinated by this. And the more I observed my dogs, the more I saw how this issue permeated almost every important aspect of their behaviour.

I noticed, for instance, how the dogs would go through a dramatic ritual whenever they came together again after being separated. I remember taking Sasha to the vet for an injection and watching her perform a ritualized licking of her housemates when she got home to Sandy, Khan and Kim.

The dogs' reaction to the appearance of strangers at the door was fascinating too. As my visitors arrived, the pack would crowd around me and the newcomers. They would be animated and interacting with each other again. Only this time they were somehow including me in this ritual. Something was going on.

That it was, in part, to do with leadership was reinforced at playtime, where Sasha was particularly to the fore. I loved playing ball with them in the wide open spaces. They would all run in the direction of the ball when I threw it. But it was Sasha who would retrieve it and bring it back to me. Heaven help any of the others if they got in the way. It was clearly an evolving, fluid situation at this time and it was interesting to observe the shifting dynamics of the different relationships. Sasha's attempts to impose herself on her older peers seemed to have proven largely successful.

Sandy's body language said it all. Around Sasha she was slouched, submissive. Her health was giving way by now and she had given up the fight. Khan remained the elder of the pack, the *éminence grise*. But there was no question in my mind that Sasha was becoming the top dog. She seemed to have assumed superiority over me too, judging by the way she blocked me from ever leaving the house before her on a walk and leapt in front of me like some presidential bodyguard whenever we heard an unexpected noise or met another dog outdoors. In this respect, she reminded me of Shane, my first canine protector. I was determined to get to the bottom of this. For a while, however, I was distracted again.

It was my horse, Raffie, who led me to my new home.

I had placed him in a livery stables in the village of Roxby but was tiring of the long drive to and from my mother and father's house. I was looking for a place somewhere nearer. While out riding with Raffie, I had taken to keeping a look-out for 'For Sale' signs. Often we'd travel five or six miles between the small villages of rural north Lincolnshire scouting for potential properties.

It was while riding down Cemetery Road on the edge of the historic market town of Winterton that I came across a house that seemed to suit my needs perfectly. It was a roomy, three-bedroomed semi, with a reasonable-sized garden. The major selling point was that it backed on to swathes of open countryside. I was in a good position to move. I still had the proceeds of my house in Brigg and immediately put my parents' home on the market. Soon the house was mine.

Money was still tight. But Wendy Broughton, along with her husband and son, John and Dan, offered to move me in their horse lorry. Good friends that they were, they mucked in for the day, shifting my furniture up and down stairs in return for a fish and chip supper when we had finished. Goodness knows what the neighbours thought of the unlikely removals van. I was too busy to care.

By the time I moved there, my pack had been reduced to just a trio of dogs. Sasha, Khan and Kim were all that remained. Old age had finally caught up with Sandy. Another dear friend gone.

Buying and selling a house is, as everyone knows, an all-consuming process. I hadn't stopped thinking about the behaviour I had been watching within my pack. But I had been forced to ease up on the reading and research I was doing.

It was, predictably, Sasha who kick-started things again.

In appearance, Sasha always reminded me of a wolf. At some point I'd had a conversation with someone who'd made the same observation. 'Well, shepherds as a breed are probably closer to their ancient ancestor than most other domestic dogs,' I'd found myself saying. Afterwards I started thinking about that. 'Of course.'

I was taken aback when I started reading books and studying wildlife videos about the dog's ancestor. Suddenly, there in the textbooks and on the television screen I was seeing wild animals replicating the same sort of ritualistic behaviour that I'd seen my own domestic dogs displaying since Sasha's arrival.

Within the wolf pack there was no confusion about leadership, it was the role of the Alpha male and his partner the Alpha female. As I studied the interaction between the Alphas and the rest of the pack, it became clear to me that this ritualistic behaviour took place at particular occasions within the pack's day-to-day routine. Specifically it happened when they were ready to go on the hunt, at meal times, when the pack came together again after a separation and when it was faced with an external threat. This in turn led me to the next big breakthrough.

Dogs have, of course, evolved in a myriad ways from their ancient ancestor. But it seemed to me that while the dog had been taken out of the wolf pack, the instincts of the wolf pack hadn't been taken out of the dog. The more I thought about it, the more obvious it became that when Sasha was blocking and balking me before and during our walks, she was actually protecting me. That was her instinct. And I began to see why. Slowly I realized that I – like every other owner – was projecting human assumptions on to the situation. I was taking it for granted that, because I was in human terms the 'leader' of the household, the dog accepted this too. But what if it didn't? What if, based on the language it understood, it believed it was leader? Suddenly I saw that this turned the entire world on its head. It would mean that a dog's 'bad' behaviour – such as the well-known phenomenon of separation anxiety – was down not to its fear of being separated from its guardians, but rather to its paranoia at being separated from members of the pack for which it was responsible.

It's amazing how a muddle of different ideas and pieces of information can slowly, almost imperceptibly coalesce into a single theory. I can't remember the moment it happened exactly. There was no bolt of lightning in the Lincolnshire sky, no Newtonian apple had dropped at my feet. But soon after arriving in Winterton I'd boiled all these disparate thoughts down into a theory. It was nowhere near perfect, I knew that. But it had a shape and a logic that made total sense to me. I knew that the key to developing a communication language lay in imposing myself as leader and doing it at the four key moments: meal times, during the walk, during times of perceived danger and whenever we were reunited after a separation. I also knew that the only way I was going to improve it was by putting it into practice.

One wet autumn morning I came downstairs determined to put my idea for a new way of communicating with my dogs to the test. In many ways, I was glad I was on my own at the time. I was convinced, rightly as it turned out, that people would just think I was being stupid. Perhaps they were right. But I wanted to find out for myself first.

The only people I let in on my intentions were Tony and Wendy.

Wendy's help was crucial. While I was developing ideas at home with my own dogs, she was applying them to her two pets, a Jack Russell called Charlie and a boxer, Katie.

She would call me up regularly. 'What are you doing with them now?' she'd ask. 'How can I do that?'

The change was mirrored in my own pack. Each of my dogs had its own problems. Kim, for instance, was terrified of thunder. Since I'd begun trying my new ideas out, she had calmed down tremendously. It became a spiral. The calmer they were, the calmer I was. And the calmer they saw me being, the calmer still they became. It was tremendous to behold.

What was really encouraging was the feedback I was getting from Wendy. She used to walk another Jack Russell for a friend. It was a very nervous and sometimes aggressive dog. As she followed my lead, the dog calmed down hugely.

'He's become a really happy chappie,' Wendy told me.

If I had a goal that single sentence summed it up. My aim was to eliminate all the violence and force that had – for generations – characterized man's relationship with the dog. To make the world a little more pleasant for every dog, and its owner. It really was music to my ears.

Chapter 21

'Every Dog Deserves a Fireplace'

As I drove through the countryside on one of the coldest mornings of the year, the Lincolnshire landscape looked more starkly and strangely beautiful than I'd ever seen it. The distorted, spidery silhouettes of the oak trees were spread like lacework across the metallic sky. A light dusting of frost had turned the muddy fields into an eerie, lunar landscape. Winterton's name was apparently derived from the ancient Anglian for 'town of winterings'. On mornings like this I could see why the season had provoked such a powerful association all those hundreds of years ago. I still think it looks at its best on bleak midwinter days like these.

I was on my way to the sanctuary to see Miss D. I arrived to find her very busy so, as was my habit by now, I took a stroll around the kennels.

Looking back, I can see that I was in quite an emotional state at the time. A few days earlier I had suffered another blow. I had lost Khan. Of all the dogs I'd had over the years, Khan was probably the most beautiful and good-natured. He was a proud, masculine yet gentle soul. As well as being a great companion, he had contributed to some of my happiest memories too. Our successes together at Cruft's were something I knew I'd never forget. I would never really get over losing him.

Normally I walked around the sanctuary with real relish. I loved seeing the new arrivals and hearing about their progress. But with the shadow of my loss still hanging over me, my anticipation was tempered with sadness. It was not a new face I wanted to see but an old and desperately missed one. Deep down, I also dreaded seeing a dog that would remind me of Khan. As it turned out, I saw something far more distressing.

I had grown accustomed to seeing some upsetting sights within the pens. But the pathetic vision that greeted me that morning still haunts me to this day.

Inside one of the blocks I saw a scrawny little white Jack Russell. He was barely more than skin and bone and had evidently been starving to death. His ribcage protruded so clearly it looked as if it was going to poke through his paper-thin coat at any moment. He was also shivering but it was nothing to do with the biting cold. It was obvious he was a bundle of nerves.

He became agitated the moment I arrived, summoning the energy from somewhere to yelp and leap around. The expression in his eyes was one of pure, unbridled terror.

I felt a powerful wave of emotion washing over me too. But it was not terror in my case, but pure, seething anger. How on God's earth had this dog been reduced to such a state? What sort of person could have done this inhumane thing to it? I stopped myself from imagining the cruelty this poor creature must have suffered. I must confess, however, I failed to prevent myself from thinking about what

I would do to the person responsible if I ever met them.

I was in such a state of shock I hardly noticed Dave arriving on my shoulder.

'Poor little bugger,' he said, in his usual blunt-as-a-blunderbuss manner. 'If I ever got my hands on the . . .' As his voice trailed away he raised a clenched fist to the air. The look I flashed told him I knew exactly what he meant.

For a while we just stood there in silence. But then Dave filled me in on what little he knew about this tragic new arrival.

Owners deliver their dogs to the sanctuary in the most appalling ways. The 'kinder' ones leave them tied up at the front gates. Others toss them over the six-foot perimeter fence. This dog's owners couldn't even be bothered to do that.

The Jack Russell had been found miles away on derelict land, abandoned and tied to a concrete block by a piece of baling twine. I knew rescue dogs suffered severe psychological damage. Some, tragically, never recover from the treatment they have received. Dave said that he and Miss D. feared this one was too far gone to be saved. He kept running off and was aggressive when approached. They were certain he would bite anyone who came too close.

Even sanctuaries have to deal in the realities of life. There was every chance this dog would have to be destroyed.

I can now see that I was emotionally at a point where I wouldn't be able to resist helping a dog like this. The loss of Khan had left a gaping void at home. I hadn't travelled to the sanctuary with the idea of finding a replacement, but that's what I found myself suggesting.

'Let me take him,' I said.

Dave was taken aback. He gave me a look as if to say: 'Don't be so daft.'

But I had never been so sure of anything. I looked at the Jack Russell and then back at Dave. 'Remember, every dog deserves a fireplace,' I smiled. 'And I think this one deserves one more than most.'

He smiled back and shrugged his shoulders. 'It's up to you.'

When I eventually saw Miss D. her reaction was no different to Dave's.

'Are you sure, my dear?' she said in her usual, diplomatic way. 'He's rather a lot to take on, don't you think?'

In truth, relations between me and Miss D. had become more strained since I began developing my ideas. She had made it clear she didn't really agree with what I was doing. In fact, she said she was very, very sceptical. I think she believed my wolf pack theory was a bit fanciful. She also had the idea that I was simply another behaviourist and didn't hide her disdain for that approach. Unlike some, at least, she was ever so polite about it. But it stung, I admit.

It hadn't kept me away from the sanctuary. I still helped out with the annual open day and ran puppy playgroups. But there was no hiding the slight distance that had grown between us.

One thing she didn't doubt, however, was my love for animals. She clearly reckoned that I probably represented this little chap's last chance. Like Dave she shrugged and said: 'It's up to you.'

But I don't think she was very happy about me taking the dog.

When I arrived home my two other dogs, Sasha and Kim, reacted warily to the newcomer. But it was the Jack Russell's behaviour that worried me most. The moment it arrived in the house it ran to the kitchen table where it hid, cowering and shivering in the shadows. If I went anywhere near, it created the most almighty commotion.

There was something almost crazy about the way he behaved. I found myself giving him a name that reflected this: Barmie.

I had achieved some success with my new method, but this represented a challenge of an entirely different dimension. For a while, I wondered whether it was me who had gone mad in deciding to take on a dog that was so damaged. Yet I knew I had to try.

Central to my thinking was the idea that dogs must be willing, ready and able to make decisions of their own free will. And to be able to do this they had to be relaxed. As I set off into the unknown, I was sure that I was going to achieve nothing until Barmie had calmed down.

I knew instinctively that this would take a long time: and so it proved. For the first few days, the most I could hope for was that Barmie would emerge from under his table and accept some food. I achieved this effectively by ignoring him all the time. I felt slightly bad about doing so. But I told myself, 'Look, this dog has suffered God-only-knows what treatment in the past.' He was terrified of his own shadow. If he was going to get his confidence back, he had to do so at his own speed and on his own terms. 'Jan, just leave him be,' I chided myself whenever I became impatient.

It was a long, long haul – but eventually Barmie overcame

his fear and emerged into the house. As he did so I slowly forged a bond with him. At first this was little more than offering a warm 'Hello' to him. As time went on I was able to offer food reward.

I had no model upon which to base this approach. This was the most severely traumatized dog I'd encountered. I had to make each day's programme up as I went along. The turning point came one bright day in the late spring when I was out in the garden.

Barmie appeared with a toy in his mouth. Within minutes he and I were playing a retrieval game. The ice had been broken.

It took many weeks of hard work to take things on from here. Mentally Barmie made huge strides. (Physically he continued to need close medical monitoring for the rest of his life. His body, and his lungs in particular, had suffered so much during his darkest days he needed daily doses of steroids.) But, to my delight, he seemed like a dog that had rediscovered his faith in people – and in life itself.

It was some months later that I was making another visit to the sanctuary. For the first time since I had found him there, I took Barmie along with me.

I was pleased that – despite all the terrible associations he would have had with arriving here – he didn't react to being back within the sanctuary's walls. Dave was delighted to see him. 'Here's a reformed character,' he said.

I urgently needed to speak to Miss D. that day so we made a beeline for her office.

She was away from her desk when we got there. Barmie was by now so lively he jumped straight up on to her chair where he made himself comfortable.

Miss D. was not a woman for great displays of affection or emotion. Not towards humans, at least. But when she appeared in the doorway the sight of this rejuvenated animal stopped her in her tracks. She went over to him and started stroking him.

'Well, young man,' she said in her usual, impeccable manner. 'That's a big change in you.'

And then she said something that almost reduced me to tears. 'If it wasn't for Jan, you wouldn't be here now. So you be good to her.'

It was only the briefest of remarks, but it was a moment of huge significance. I knew I wasn't going to convert her completely to my ideas. She was too long in the tooth for that, I think. Too proud too, most likely. But I'm sure she took my work much more seriously from then on. She certainly knew that I was doing some good. And that meant a great deal to me.

Chapter 22

'That's a Turn-Up'

Outside the night sky was starless and the gusts of gale-force wind driving in from the North Sea were so strong they were pitching my elderly jalopy of a vehicle all over the narrow lanes.

It was no more hospitable inside my latest car, an 'ever so humble' grey Ford I'd christened The Heap. True to recent form, on one of the coldest nights of the year its erratic old heater had refused to work.

As it happened, driving through the pitch-black country-side that night, I was all but oblivious to the sub-zero cold. I was far more concerned with the nervous knot in my stomach and the nagging question that had put it there: 'What on earth am I getting myself into here?'

I was on the way to the small coastal village of Barrow-on-Humber, to visit a friend of my son Tony. She'd heard Tony talking about the successes I'd been having with my method and had asked him whether I'd have a look at her dog, a high-combustion collie cross called Pepsi. Pepsi was proving a handful and she confessed she'd be grateful for any help going in improving the dog's behaviour. I'd said yes, almost instinctively. 'What harm can I do?' I had thought to myself.

Almost immediately, however, the doubts had begun to creep in. Now, as I approached their house at the village, I was belatedly beginning to qualify my own question. 'What harm can I do? Apart, that is, from turning myself into the local laughing stock.'

Barrow-on-Humber is a small collection of houses on the edge of the Humber estuary separating north Lincolnshire and Yorkshire. It's an exposed spot, but a picturesque little place nevertheless, dotted with houses and cottages made of traditional stone and slate. (It was in one of these houses that the village's most famous son, the great English clockmaker John Harrison, solved the age-old longitude problem.)

Tony's friends lived on the edge of the village, in a lovely old terraced house. I pulled up outside, took a deep breath and readied myself for the jump into the deep end.

As entrances go, my debut as a troubleshooting trainer was hardly auspicious. Elizabeth Taylor in *Cleopatra* it was not. The wind was so ferocious it was a real struggle to fight my way from the car to the front door. I had a heavy coat on and had to pull the hood right over my head as I leaned into the storm. As the door opened, I must have looked like I'd been dragged through a hedge backwards, particularly to this lady, a leading light in the local Women's Institute, who looked immaculate.

It was around 7.30 p.m. as I walked in. I remember because her husband's favourite television programme, *Coronation Street*, was starting. It was clear I was not about to distract him from it.

He was in the living room, lying on a luxurious six-foot sofa. He had clearly not been home from work for long. He was still wearing a pinstripe suit and a tie. My arrival in his front room was greeted with the cursory raising of an arm, partly because he was more interested in his programme and partly because I think he assumed I was another of his wife's friends from the WI, round to swap recipes for shortcake or pencil in the details for the next whist drive.

I saw that the husband was also restraining a dog on the sofa. 'This is Pepsi,' his wife said, semi-apologetically. A few moments later we were joined by their fourteen-year-old daughter, who looked understandably wary of the strange goings on.

If I am honest, I had walked into this situation without a clear game plan. And I made my apprehensiveness clear from the word go. 'My method works for me, but it may not work for you,' I remember saying on more than one occasion during those nervous first minutes.

Common sense told me, however, that I had to get a measure of the problem first. So the first thing I did was ask the husband to let Pepsi go.

It was easy to see why they had asked for outside help. She used her owner's chest as a springboard and launched herself like a rocket into the air. She then proceeded to run and leap around the room, barking incessantly.

Pepsi wasn't aggressive in any way. She was friendly but frantic. I could see immediately that this wasn't exuberance or high spirits, the standard explanation for such behaviour. Just by looking at her vivid, darting eyes I could see Pepsi was scared of something. If there is one thing guaranteed to stir my emotions, it is the sight of an unhappy dog. The moment I saw those eyes I knew I had to try my ideas out.

In the years since, I have delivered the same speech hundreds of times. As I found the words coming out of my mouth for the first time that night, however, I was terrified of being laughed out of the room.

Few people had ever listened to me before, so I was very unsure. I kept asking them whether it made sense. They just nodded quietly.

Still slightly unsure of myself, I went on to explain that I was going to remove the job of leader from Pepsi. I was, in effect, going to stage a bloodless coup.

I set to work applying two elements of my method in particular. With the husband still engrossed in his television show, I asked the mother and daughter to begin acting like leaders by ignoring the subordinate pack member that was their dog, putting into practice what I later called the five-minute rule. Fortunately, they hadn't given Pepsi her evening meal. So I also asked them to assert their authority here, by using the technique I call gesture eating, essentially letting the dog see them eating before giving out its meal.

Results came quite quickly. The first good sign was a noticeable calming in Pepsi. Encouraged by this I got her to sit. They told me this was something that normally took about six attempts. I did it in one.

At one point, the daughter left her chair in the living room to go to the kitchen. Her mother told me that Pepsi always followed her there, but this time she remained in her spot. These were all good, positive developments.

It was hard to know what was more satisfying, however:

the transformation in Pepsi or in the lady's husband. At first he had continued watching the television, seemingly lost in his soap opera. After a while, however, I noticed he had the remote control in his hand and was surreptitiously lowering the volume a notch or two every now and again.

As things developed with Pepsi, he turned his body so that he was propped up on one elbow and could steal glances. By the end of the first hour, he was sitting on the edge of the sofa, head in cupped hand, elbows on knees, silently watching the events unfolding. The television was by now switched off.

He wasn't a man of many words. 'Hmmm. That's a turn-up,' he muttered on one or two occasions. But to be honest he didn't need to say anything. I could see the results I was getting and that was more than enough.

It was closing in on midnight when I eventually left them. As I headed back out the door, Pepsi was lying on the carpet by the embers of the fire, settled in for what was clearly going to be a good night's sleep.

I couldn't resist feeling pleased with myself. As I walked out of the house, smiling inwardly as I battled with the winds once more, I remember thinking to myself: 'Well that made 'em look.'

Now I know differently, of course, but at the time, it didn't seem like a life-changing moment. I certainly didn't think I had found a new vocation in life. Driving back to Winterton, I was pleased things had worked out so well. More than anything, I was relieved that I hadn't made a fool of myself.

Looking back, though, perhaps I should have read the

runes and spotted that something significant was happening, that – above the blanket of coal-black clouds – some strange alignment in my stars was at work. The clearest sign of all came a mile or so down the road. Out in the open country once more, I felt a sudden – and very unfamiliar – surge of warm air coursing through the car. Even The Heap's heating had suddenly decided to behave a little better.

Chapter 23

Miracle Worker

The heart of Winterton was a village straight out of a novel by one of the Brontë sisters. An old market square, hemmed in by a collection of solid, greystone houses. A handful of lead-windowed shops and two pubs. A Norman church spire overlooking it all. It was easy to imagine the village having looked this way for centuries. And life certainly ran to the same rhythms that it did a hundred years ago. The annual agricultural show was still the highlight of the social calendar.

In a small, sleepy community like Winterton, word of even the most minor events spreads fast. So it was inevitable that the corner-shop chatterboxes and pub gossips were soon having a chuckle at the tales of 'miracle cures' happening on their doorstep. I never got to hear the stories, although I know they existed. I'm sure they were strange and highly entertaining, particularly after a few hours in the bar. The shame was they could never have matched the curious, sometimes comic reality of the new life that was now opening up to me.

My success with Pepsi gave me a lot of encouragement.

Her owners were very complimentary and slowly others began to ask me for help. It soon became apparent that I would have to use my imagination to deal with the diverse and sometimes downright odd situations that I would face.

One of the first calls came from a district nurse called Sally. Sally lived with her four-year-old mongrel, Bruce, in a village nearby. Sally and Bruce were devoted to each other. The problem was that Bruce in particular was a little too devoted. Whenever Sally went to work he would trash the house, rolling her clothes up into a makeshift bed and eating away at the frame of the front door.

It was a classic case of separation anxiety, something I would face again and again. The solution, however, was unique. The key to Sally's problems, as far as I was concerned, lay in the drama that she was attaching to her daily departure to work. I understood how close she was to Bruce. She told me she had recently separated from her partner and had come to rely on Bruce as her greatest source of companionship and love. No one could relate to that more than I.

Yet Sally was creating a huge disruption when she left home each day. One minute there would be a television or a radio blaring away, the next she'd be fussing over Bruce, going out the door and leaving him in a house full of silence. It was no wonder he was going crazy, particularly when he had clearly come to think that he was Sally's greatest friend and protector in the world.

I'll never forget my surprise when Sally suggested her novel solution. 'I know, I could go out of the living-room window.' I had told her that one of the keys to easing

Bruce's anxiety was taking the focus of those anxieties away from the front door. Like so many of the people who asked me to help them in those early days, she was absolutely determined to solve her dog's problems. And that meant she was willing to do anything – including entering and leaving her home through a window.

We decided to give it a go. Sally made a big production of putting on her coat in front of Bruce. She left the radio on a low volume. Barely able to suppress a fit of the giggles, she clambered out of the window. She then walked around the side of the house and duly appeared again through the front door. As she re-entered the house she listened to my advice and ignored Bruce. I wanted this to appear like an everyday moment, something that was of no concern to Bruce as a non-decision-making member of the house. That was, it has to be said, particularly hard as he was wearing an expression that neither of us would ever forget.

It was pure puzzlement. His eyes were darting back and forth from the door to Sally. 'How did you get there?' they were asking. 'You were sitting here a minute ago.'

It was now a matter of repetition. I left Sally to keep building on this. She telephoned me that weekend to tell me that Bruce had relaxed a lot. The doorway hadn't been attacked once. Sally was, she admitted, getting extremely odd looks from her neighbours as she climbed out of the window each day. But she didn't care.

The more I travelled to people's homes, the more shocked I became at the carnage misbehaving dogs could wreak. When I got a phone call from a Grimsby family about the problems they were having with their two cross-bred dogs, it sounded reasonably routine. Nothing could have prepared me for the scene I witnessed when I went round to the house, however.

My first impressions were misleading to say the least. I found the family, a husband, wife and their two children, sitting on stools in the kitchen. All was calm. There was no sign of dogs anywhere. As the father, Paul, described the problems they were having, however, it was clear there was tension in the house. I noticed he was clenching his fists as he spoke. His knuckles were turning white.

When I'd listened I asked to see the dogs. At once the entire family went into what must have been a practised routine.

'OK kids,' the father said.

The two of them climbed on to the top of the breakfast bar. The wife lifted herself higher on to her stool. Paul then went to release the dogs. He gave one final look at his wife and kids. 'Ready,' he grimaced.

'Oh boy,' I thought. 'What have we got here?'

I can only describe what happened next as an explosion. Two little dogs burst into the room and proceeded to literally bounce off the walls. It was like a circus act – except no one was finding it entertaining.

By now I was growing more and more confident that I could help almost any dog overcome its behavioural problems. But this was a test, I must admit.

It took me several hours to calm the dogs down. Paul admitted that part of the problem was that he was shouting at them. Much of my time was spent teaching him to keep his voice calm and controlled when the dogs misbehaved. Results came – slowly.

When I left that night, the atmosphere in the kitchen

was utterly different to that I'd encountered hours earlier. The two dogs were sleeping on a new bean bag that the wife had bought. She had been afraid to even produce it until now. They'd destroyed a whole succession of them in the past.

The children had gone to bed but the parents were now able to sit and drink their tea in peace. Paul's hands were no longer knotted up when he spoke. It was a hell of a transformation, I must admit.

As my casebook grew, I had come to realize that I had to be prepared for anything. Simultaneously I was realizing that my method could have quite unexpected benefits too.

It was during this time that I was asked to visit a boxer that was causing problems to a family living in the picturesque town of Gainsborough.

This was one of the first cases that had been referred to me by a vet, something I was delighted about. He had heard of the success I was having and suggested the owners give me a call. In most ways the boxer was typical of so many of the dogs I was now seeing. He was overprotective, agitated and aggressive at times. I was sure I could straighten most of his problems out – with one notable exception.

I had been in the house a short while when someone walked past the front window. This, I had been told, was the sort of everyday incident that could set the boxer off. Sure enough it was the trigger for some histrionics. He jumped up remonstrating with the passer-by, clearly wound up by the danger he sensed outside. It was as he leapt around that I suddenly became aware of a rather unpleasant aroma in the room.

The family had two teenage children. They picked it up too and reacted as you'd expect two teenagers to do. 'Oh no, not again,' they shouted, pinching their noses and waving their arms around.

'Can you do anything about the smell?' the mother asked me.

I wasn't going to lie. 'No,' I said.

I got down to work with the family and we achieved some success. I must admit I was glad to get out of the house. The dog's flatulence was a real problem and the smell was overpowering at times.

The key lesson I had learned during these early days was the importance of staying in touch and providing ongoing back-up to owners. I knew my method required dedication and that people found it hard to apply themselves continuously. An occasional pep talk on the telephone worked wonders at times. The family kept in contact over the following days and weeks.

A couple of weeks after I'd seen them, the mother rang up sounding particularly pleased.

'I'm really happy with him,' she said. 'He's calmed down completely. People are walking past the window and he's not reacting at all.'

I asked her a few questions about his behaviour. Her answers satisfied me that they were applying my method well. She was about to end the conversation when she remembered one other piece of good news.

'Oh, and by the way, we don't get so many bad smells now either,' she said.

It was only afterwards that I realized. 'Of course, they were related to each other,' I told myself.

I'd surprised myself a lot over the previous months. That was one of the more unexpected discoveries.

It was in coping with the complications of the owners' lives that the real difficulties often lay. And that was never more applicable than in the case of another devoted couple experiencing troubles together.

The call came through soon after I'd worked with Sally. The voice at the end of the line was that of an elderly lady. Her voice was quavering and she was clearly close to tears.

'We've been married forty years and we've survived so much, but this is the biggest thing that's ever come between us,' she said. 'I'm beginning to think you might be our last hope.'

In truth, the call took me by surprise. I had seen the lady and her husband around the village from time to time. They appeared one of those inseparable pairings, the kind of couple that does everything together. They even looked alike, both diminutive and greying and possessed of the gentle manners of a bygone age. That's what made the call all the more surprising – and faintly alarming.

I knew the street where they lived. A road of retirement bungalows, each with impeccably manicured lawns and bountiful borders of flowers, it was a tranquil place, even by Winterton's sleepy standards. But I had hardly set foot in their hallway, before I had sensed the tension in their house – and spotted its root cause.

The husband had owned his two-and-a-half-year-old Cairn terrier since he was a puppy. The problems had begun when his wife had fallen for a beautiful little labrador. The two dogs had simply not got along, and were snapping and snarling at each other – and occasionally their owners too.

As relations between the dogs had deteriorated, so too had those between the husband and wife. They say it's the little things that tear apart even the most solid marriages. Compared to some of the hurdles they'd overcome in forty years together it wasn't their biggest test by any stretch of the imagination. They were part of the World War II generation and had survived goodness knows what horrors in their youth. But here they were, in the twilight of their lives, at each other's throats over their dogs.

They were clearly desperate to sort the problem out and were both keen to put their side of the argument. They had adopted positions poles apart.

As far as the husband was concerned, the new dog was the root cause of the problem and would have to leave.

His wife's view was that he had not worked hard enough to make her dog welcome. She was clearly besotted with her dog and wouldn't even consider parting with it. In effect she was saying: 'Love me, love my dog.' It was heart-breaking to see two such devoted people caught up in a situation like this.

I quickly set about working with the two dogs. At first I concentrated on equalizing them, on persuading the more dominant, older dog that he was, in fact, no more deserving of leadership status than the first. I then assisted the couple to begin implementing the first elements of my method, ignoring the dogs and gesture eating. Results came quickly.

In those days, I went back to visit all my clients person-ally. It was, I suppose, a reflection of the uncertainty I was still feeling. But because so many of them were local people, it was also semi-social. I became friendly with many of those I helped. In fact I often became quite attached to them and their dogs and liked to be sure they were well. Seeing this sweet couple in such distress really got to me, so I must admit I paid them more attention than most. They worked hard at putting my ideas into practice and I was delighted when I went round and found the atmosphere in the house improved.

A few weeks after I'd first visited the couple I popped in again to see them and their two dogs. The transformation of the mood in the house was total.

I found the two dogs lying down close to each other, enjoying an afternoon siesta. They looked like two peas in a pod, like brother and sister. 'The two of them seem to like each other now,' the wife said.

I felt I'd got to know them well enough to venture what was, in retrospect, rather an impertinent question.

'And do you two like each other better too?'

It was her husband who provided the answer. He stepped towards her, wrapped an arm around her shoulder and gave her a loving squeeze.

'Let's say you've saved us a trip to the solicitors,' he said, smiling first at me and then his blushing wife. Their golden wedding anniversary must be drawing near by now . . .

Chapter 24

The Flying Flags

It was a bright May morning and the rolling, green country-side around Normanby Hall looked idyllic, like something straight out of a landscape by Constable. The huge estate, a few miles outside Scunthorpe, was one of Lincolnshire's grander spots. The imposing stately home at its heart was still home to its owner, Lord Sheffield. But part of the land was open to the public and I often rode Raffie around. I loved the open space it provided and the sight of the deer roaming its thousands of acres of lush grazing land. The pressures of making my new venture succeed sometimes got on top of me. There was nowhere better to escape them.

Today, however, I was there to do my bit as a judge at the annual Scunthorpe Horse Trials. Pressure – of a different type – was about to come my way.

I'd first become involved in the county horse-riding community via my local event, the Winterton Show.

One of the things I most enjoyed about living in the countryside was the way the community celebrated their geographical good fortune by coming together during the summer months for agricultural shows. Winterton's show, held each July, was one of the most enjoyable, not least because the showground was at the end of my road. In the period leading up to the two-day event, the road would be decked out in colourful bunting.

The event was divided into two halves: the first day was devoted to the animals, with livestock competitions and horse-riding events, the second was a giant funfair for the children. On both days the showground would be filled with tents and stalls selling home-made jams and marmalades, people demonstrating traditional country crafts like basket weaving and wood turning. It was a lovely event. There would be coconut shy stalls, motorbike displays, all sorts of attractions. I really loved it. It always reminded me of why I had been drawn to living a more rural lifestyle in the first place.

When I'd moved to the town I'd made a special effort to get involved with the show. Apart from anything else, it seemed to me like the best way to get to know people. It hadn't got off to the most auspicious start.

That first year I volunteered to help with the junior horse-riding competition. My seemingly simple job was to lead the children from the field in which they mounted their horses into the show arena. I'd never imagined something so straightforward could be so hard.

Until that day I couldn't think of anything cuter than the sight of young children astride their ponies, dressed up in their jodhpurs, riding boots, riding jacket and helmet. There was something quintessentially English about it. It conjured up memories of those wonderful cartoons by Thelwell. By the end of the same day the sight of another little girl on a horse would have given me a migraine.

When I got to the paddock about twenty little girls of different shapes and sizes were gathered there. Each was clinging with varying degrees of panic to a miniature horse. Some looked petrified, others determined. For all of them, clearly, this was a huge moment in their young lives.

If it was a big day for these International Velvets in the making, it was an even bigger one for their mothers. Even before the competition began they were fretting and fussing over every detail of their daughters' appearance, usually in a very loud voice.

'Deborah, tuck your jodhpurs into your boots, darling.'

'Elizabeth, sit up straight.'

'Mary, you look faint, dear. Do you want to come off?'

So it was to no one's surprise but my own that my first request for the girls to start moving towards the competition ring was drowned out by the din of a dozen mothers shouting at the same time.

I raised my voice the second time and got a reasonable response. I kept repeating the exercise until most of the girls had clicked their stirrups and wobbled their way towards me.

But there was one mother in particular who just wouldn't shut up. After about the umpteenth request, I snapped. 'Madam, is your daughter going to compete or not?' I asked her as sternly as I thought sensible. If looks could kill . . .

This was only the beginning of my troubles, however. Some of the girls had clearly been pushed into the competition far too early. They could barely control their ponies, poor things. What was supposed to be a poised and dignified parade towards the centrepiece of the show, quickly turned into a sort of slow motion stampede. I led as many as I could into the ring, but I couldn't guide them all. Soon the air was reverberating with cries of 'Mummy, help,' and 'Popeye, naughty horse, naughty horse, turn this way.'

One poor girl ended up heading towards the show-ground's exit and was only saved by an eagle-eyed steward. As the final pony plodded its way into the ring, I almost collapsed with relief.

I remember at that moment, I felt a gentle tap on the shoulder. I turned to see a young girl, one of the leading lights of the local horse set, offering me a large glass of orange juice.

'You look like you could do with this,' she smiled before introducing herself. 'Pushy pony club mothers. Please shoot me if I ever get to be like that.'

'Never again,' I smiled.

It was John James, the organizer of the Winterton Show horse events – and many others in the county – who involved me in judging more serious competitions. I'd got talking to him at the Winterton Show and he'd invited me to be a judge on the cross-country course at a meeting to be held in Caister. That had passed off without any major incident. So now he'd asked me to help out again. Hence my presence at Normanby Hall.

This was a different league, however. The Scunthorpe Horse Trials attracted some of the best riders not only in the country but the world. The Olympic champion Mark Todd and the Flying Scot, Ian Stark, were among the stars who rode there.

I arrived at Normanby Hall and joined the rest of the judges for the morning briefing. John asked me to act as the judge at one of the fences out on the cross-country course.

It consisted of poles set at an angle on a corner of the course. It was a tricky jump and demanded the utmost concentration on the part of horse and rider.

At the really big shows, judges communicated with each other by radio or walkie-talkie. John James and one or two of his senior judges had them, but they didn't have enough to go around. Like every judge, however, I had the standard set of four coloured equestrian flags to indicate any problems. It was red for a doctor, blue for a vet, white for a fence to be rebuilt and orange for stop the course.

It didn't take me long to get myself embroiled in controversy. Early on during the morning, I watched a woman rider approaching on a horse. As far as I – and everyone else watching – was concerned, the horse was running along really well. As she got closer, however, I realized that the rider was violently using her stick on the horse. Riders are obviously allowed to use a little force in steering their mounts, but this was wrong. It wasn't necessary and even if it had been it was clearly excessive. As far as I was concerned, the rider was effectively beating up the horse.

When I handed in my result sheet, I put a note on the side of the form. 'Used the stick'. It was enough to get the rider disqualified.

During a break in riding the girl's mother came storming up to the judges' tent. 'Right, which bloody judge was responsible for this?' she said in a threatening manner. John

James was a quintessential English gentleman, impeccably mannered and correct in everything he did. He dealt with the situation with his usual smoothness.

'Madam, the judge concerned is highly responsible and was correct for asking for disqualification,' he said. She gave him a look like thunder, but knew that to challenge him might lead to even more trouble. I had been happy to face up to her. But I was glad that he backed me up in that way.

The day continued without any major incident. I think I'd thrown up the white flag for the fence to be rebuilt two or three times. Then another female rider approached and got it completely wrong. She misjudged it hopelessly and the horse ploughed into the middle of the fence at speed. The force of the collision sent the fence crashing, but more worryingly both horse and rider were sent flying. The rider was thrown clear of the fence into the soft grass and landed unhurt. The horse, however, was knocked sideways and fell awkwardly. I feared the worst.

Of course my job that afternoon was to keep my corner of the course in contact with the main control tent. I knew I needed to signal something – but what? Any of the flags would have done. So I simply threw them all in the air.

My main concern was in making sure horse and rider were OK. Well, that's not exactly the case. To be honest, my greatest fear was that the horse had seriously hurt itself. So I headed for it first.

It was only afterwards that I thought about it. I was fairly certain that the rider had landed safely and had probably suffered nothing more than wounded pride. But I didn't know for sure.

One of the fun elements of the show was the post-mortem that took place afterwards, often over a glass of something home-brewed at one of the beer and produce tents. There were always amusing incidents to talk about. This year the sight of my flying flags seemed to have caused most of the mirth. It turned out the girl was a member of one of the area's leading landowning families.

I should have guessed then that one of the first phone calls I would get the following week was from the same family. For a moment I thought they were going to inform me of legal proceedings or something. In fact, the woman at the other end of the line was asking for my advice.

'I gather you're rather good at sorting out wayward dogs,' she said. 'I've got a pair who are giving me real headaches. Could you spare some time to have a look?'

I must admit that as I steered up their gravel drive to the front door, I was a little concerned.

I needn't have fretted. The woman was the sister of the rider I'd seen come a cropper at the show a few weeks earlier. She was more interested in her dogs, a German shepherd and a Jack Russell. They weren't getting on at all and had started biting each other. She listened intently to what I said. 'How clever,' she smiled. She said she'd give my method a go. 'Can't do any harm, can it?'

I'd been there for a couple of hours when, despite my best efforts to steer the conversation away from the subject, she started talking about the show.

She said her sister was a very keen horse rider. 'I heard the flags were flying that day, weren't they?' she smiled.

I thought I'd better come clean. So I explained it had been me that had been involved.

'I'm sorry, I looked after the horse first,' I said.

I'd already sensed what her reaction was going to be, but it was good to hear it nevertheless. 'Oh, you were quite right. My sister was fine, the fall probably did her good. The horse was far more important.' We got on like a house on fire from then onwards.

Chapter 25

Radio Waves

'Jan, your next caller has a problem with an aggressive rabbit.'

My life has taken its share of unexpected turns, but there were few to match the one that led to me sitting in a radio studio and taking telephone calls like that.

It was the winter of 1996 and I had begun a regular slot on BBC Radio Humberside, helping people deal with their problem pets. The road that led me here was a curious one, to say the least.

By now I was delving deeper into dog behaviour and a new way of communicating with them. In the wake of my breakthrough observing wolves, I was open to all sorts of ideas. I had made great strides by keeping an open mind. I wasn't going to stop now. So when I saw an advert in a dog newspaper for people to contribute to a project to find out whether dogs were psychic, I decided to write in.

The more I studied dogs, the more impressed I became with their intelligence. They were clearly much more capable and cognitive thinkers than most people had ever given them credit for. The advert made me think about something that puzzled me. I'd noticed my dogs' uncanny ability to know almost intuitively when I was going to take them out for a walk. I would mentally decide it was time for a stroll then discover that – even before I got my coat and shoes on – the dogs were in an incredibly excited state. I'd eliminated obvious explanations like the time of day. My life was far from routine at that time and there was no particular pattern to when we'd go for a walk. I didn't know what the explanation was. So I wrote a letter basically saying, if they are psychic then this might be proof of it. It was partly in fun, but I was intrigued when I received a letter back saying the research was being carried out for a BBC television programme, *Out of this World*. The producers came to see me and they asked me to set up an experiment with cameras trained on the dogs and on me.

I was determined to be as scientific as I could. I'd make a note of the time when I mentally decided I was ready to go for a walk, then compare the timed video footage to see what the dogs were doing at that precise moment. I was amazed to see that the dogs did get restless at the same time. I know it sounds strange and slightly wacky, but this is what happened. The producer was delighted with the footage and a few weeks later told me that it would feature on the show, presented by Carol Vorderman.

It was during the run-up to the broadcast that I was called by BBC Radio Humberside.

They'd been told that I was going to feature on national television and wanted to run an interview with me. They sent a reporter down and we recorded a piece. We obviously spoke about the item for the show. We treated it very much in a tongue-in-cheek way. I didn't know what the explanation was, nor was I going to speculate. It seemed inexplicable. The reporter who came to see me was interested in dogs so we carried on talking. He mentioned how calm and happy my dogs seemed to be. So I told him about the work I was doing, helping people in the area with problem dogs.

'I think the listeners would love to hear more about that,' he said. 'I'll have a word with the producer and see if we can get you in to do something else.'

Sure enough, a few days later I got a call from a producer, asking me whether I could do a phone-in one morning in November at 9 a.m. The idea was that listeners would ring in with assorted pet-related problems and I'd offer advice. I was going to be a dog version of one of my favourite television characters. Perhaps they should have called me Frasier Cranine.

A thousand butterflies were fluttering around my stomach the morning I drove to the studios for the first show. Most of the people I knew listened to the local station and would hear me that day. I was fixated with the idea of them sitting there waiting for me to make a slip-up. At one point, I thought about turning the car around and giving up on it. Yet I sensed it was a gold-plated opportunity for me. One I had to take.

The DJ, Jeremy Buxton, was great in easing my nerves. But they quickly returned when I saw the control board light up with callers after he introduced me. I was hoping the first call would be a positive one. I couldn't have wished for a better start. The call was from a man whose dog kept running off. 'He'll just bolt away for no reason. We've tried everything, and it's not as if we're not giving him enough exercise,' he said, sounding exasperated.

I knew the key to making this work was to connect with people, to make them feel I understood. Here was a scenario I recognized all too well. So I began by recounting my own tragic experience with Purdey. From the sympathetic noises he was making, I think he realized that I knew how he was feeling. I then gave him advice on how vital it was to build on the walk from the beginning, and to practise his controls at home before going out with the dog again. 'Well, it's food for thought,' he said at the end of the call.

The show had presented me as an expert on all pets. I must admit my heart sank when the next call came through and it was the mother of a little boy who was having trouble with his rabbit. 'It keeps nipping at him,' she explained.

On the way to the studio I had decided that in the absence of a specific answer to a question I should apply simple common sense.

'What's your son doing to the rabbit when this happens?' I asked, suspecting I knew the answer.

'It's usually when he's picking it up out of the cage,' she said.

'Well, there's your problem. The rabbit sees that as an attack on him,' I replied. 'He's not doing it deliberately, but your son's hurting the rabbit and the animal is retaliating. Ask him how he'd like it if you picked him out of bed as roughly as that in the morning?'

I suggested that her son start trying to coax the rabbit out of its hutch instead, rewarding it with food and affection when it did so. She went away seemingly pleased and intent on giving it a go.

Thankfully, however, most of the calls were from dog owners.

What hit me most even during that first session was how desperate people were. I remember one woman was convinced her dog was punishing her by chewing the furniture in her home. No matter how hard I tried to get her to see she was misguided, she kept going back to the idea that the dog was taking it out on her. 'What have I done to him?' she kept saying. It was frustrating to have to end a call, knowing that I hadn't got through.

I have never known thirty minutes fly by so quickly. It seemed to be over before we'd even started. We'd only got through six calls. At the end, as I talked to the producer, I was told that there had been another twenty callers waiting to talk to me.

'Can you come back and do another one?' the producer asked.

And so I started a regular slot. Before long the time was being extended to a full hour. I absolutely loved it, I must say. Apart from the sheer fun it provided, it gave me immense satisfaction when I heard people reacting positively to what I was saying. I was pleased too when people started calling back with positive results. Even the mother of the boy with the rabbit rang in again to say my suggestion had worked a treat. It gave me still more confidence to develop my ideas. In truth, I was finding new ways of expressing those ideas almost every time I went on the air.

Of course, not everyone agreed with the direction I was going in. On air, there was the odd caller who made it plain they thought I was talking poppycock. That wasn't new. Some friends had expressed their discomfort with the ideas I was expressing so openly now. Others kept a diplomatic silence, but couldn't disguise their disapproval. Miss D. at the JG Sanctuary was still among those whose silence spoke volumes.

Nevertheless, it hadn't really occurred to me that people would feel violently opposed to my ideas. Until, that was, one day when I returned from the radio station. I'd just completed an hour-long phone-in. It had been as much fun as ever. The callers had been the usual mixture of dog and cat lovers, kids with caterpillars and parents wanting advice on how to choose a hamster for a Christmas present. By now, however, dog owners made up the overwhelming majority of my callers.

The more I spoke publicly about my ideas, the more rounded my argument became and the more confident I was on air. I felt almost evangelical about my belief in non-violence and the possibilities of humans and dogs living in peaceful co-existence. And at times this came out over the airwaves.

I was arriving at the door when I saw a familiar figure approach. It was a man who lived a couple of doors down from me. I barely knew him. All that had really registered about him was that he had a golden retriever, which he exercised in the park where I took my dogs. He was a quiet, mind-my-own-business man. In short, a typical Lincolnshire character.

What I saw that morning, however, was someone completely different. He rushed towards me, an ugly look on his face, clearly angry.

'You're telling lies, you're conning people you are,' he shouted, waving his arms animatedly. 'You should be horsewhipped so that you shut up.' I was so shocked by the vehemence of this verbal onslaught that I froze to the spot. I was backing into the porch, wondering how far he was going to go. He was soon turning back towards his home. But he left with a parting shot. 'Don't worry, we'll stop you from spreading your evil,' he said.

I was stunned. I got inside and slid down the wall of the hallway. I was in a state of shock. Sasha and Barmie were there. As ever, they protected me, cuddling up to me as the sobs began.

His words kept churning around in my mind for the next couple of hours. Being accused of telling lies had always been an emotive issue with me. I had suffered it at school when I'd claimed my great-uncle worked with Buffalo Bill and again when I said I had a brother. To have that levelled at me again hurt deeply. But it was the other inferences that cut deepest. Who was I conning? The dogs, the owners? And what was I gaining from it all? I hadn't earned a penny for my appearances, not even petrol expenses. The word that kept resonating inside me, however, was that I was spreading evil.

I was trying to make the world a less violent place. How could that be evil?

Tony came home that night and helped me get over the shock. Since an early age he had displayed a wisdom way beyond his years. He also knew what made me tick probably better than anyone else. Not for the first – or last – time he said the right thing.

'Mum, you're on to something here,' he said. 'All your

life people have been trying to shut you up. You're not going to let someone like that do it to you again?'

He was right, of course. But it was sometimes easier said than done.

Chapter 26

Doubting Thomases

Spring was in the air and I arrived early at Raffie's livery stables to find a familiar figure delivering hay. 'If it isn't the dog expert. Still trying to push those new-fangled ideas?' he said with a jaunty smile.

A big-boned, ruddy-faced farmer and landowner, decked out in his padded green coat and flat tweed cap, his name was Pete. In many ways he summed up the sort of resistance I was beginning to face in the area.

Like many of his fellow farmers, Pete came from a family that had worked the surrounding land for generations. As far as he was concerned I was an outsider – and, what was worse, an outsider with ideas.

If I was being charitable, I could understand some of his misgivings. The notion of a southerner – and even worse a southern woman – coming up to their neck of the woods and claiming she understood animals better than they did would have been hard for men like Pete to stomach. But that was their problem, not mine.

By now, I was beginning to think my training might one day make me a living. And in the wake of the talking-to

Tony had given me after my neighbour's verbal attack, I had decided it was time to stand up for myself. So that's what I did.

'Well, your grandfather would have asked you the same question,' I said, nodding at the new, gadget-laden tractor he was driving.

Pete looked baffled. 'What are you on about?' he said.

'Well, he probably had a horse pulling his hay-cart. He'd have thought that tractor was a new-fangled idea.'

He shot me a look as if to say, 'Don't be clever with me,' then headed off to unload some hay. I was sorting out my tack and hung around.

While he was away I noticed the lovely little Jack Russell that travelled everywhere with him. Whenever his 'master' was off his tractor, the dog would take up a position on the driver's seat and bark incessantly.

Pete reappeared to find me looking at his dog. 'So go on then, tell me why he's doing that,' he said with a defiant tilt of his head.

The unspoken challenge was clear: 'You think you're so clever, explain my dog to me.'

'Simple,' I said. 'He's just doing his job. Unless you tell them otherwise, all dogs think they're leader of their pack. He thinks he's responsible for you, and he's protecting his territory. But he's also agitated that you're not there. How would you like it if your child just disappeared without a word of warning?'

For a moment he was quiet. You could almost hear the gears in his brain turning over. I half expected to hear the sound of a penny dropping.

No sooner had the thought settled into his head, however, than his face had turned to thunder. He didn't have a response so he just waved his arm at me, as if I was some pesky fly to be swatted away.

'Ah, get away with you,' he said, clambering up on to the seat of his tractor.

It was a small but important victory. No words were exchanged. But it didn't matter. I knew – and he knew – that I'd made him think.

Entrenched views like that weren't hard to find, that's for sure. Often they were expressed more subtly, as they were when I went to see a wealthy businessman one evening in the town of Burton upon Stather. He and his wife had asked me in to look at their wayward labrador.

He was the managing director of a large industrial concern in the county and lived in some luxury. When I turned up he had just got back from work and was still in his suit. 'Don't mind if I pour myself a drink?' he asked. He also grabbed a packet of crisps from the bar area.

I had barely begun working when the labrador padded over to his master. He duly popped a couple of crisps into the dog's mouth.

'Sorry, but you'll have to stop that if I'm going to achieve anything,' I said as politely as I could.

His reaction was dismissive. 'Why? It's my dog.'

This was the kind of attitude I was going to have to face all the time, I knew that. There is something sacrosanct about the relationship between owner and dog. It's almost akin to that between parent and child. How would I have liked it if someone had come into my home and started telling me how to raise my children? I knew the only way

I was going to overcome it was by being firm. So that's how I proceeded.

'OK, well thanks very much, nice to have met you,' I said, grabbing my coat and making for the hallway.

'Hold on. You're here to help me get this dog sorted,' he said brusquely, as if addressing a minion at the office.

'Well, if you don't let me do my job I won't be able to help you,' I said. He didn't know it but I was shaking. I felt I could hardly stand up. Who was I to come into this man's house and start dictating like this? I was asking myself. But I couldn't show him my weakness. I had to stand my ground.

There was an awkward silence, then his wife appeared from the kitchen.

She had clearly heard what was going on. She turned to her husband. 'There you are, darling, you'll have to listen to someone for a change,' she said with a telling little smile.

That single comment told me a lot. Clearly at work – and probably at home – he was master of all he surveyed. He was used to doing what he wanted, and to having others do as he told them. Now here he was in his own living room, losing control – albeit briefly – of the creature whose obedience he took for granted more than any other, his dog. It probably didn't help that he was ceding ground to a woman, and one who didn't look as if she could afford the price of his next cigar.

He threw his hands up as if in surrender and muttered: 'OK, you win, you win.' As she returned to the kitchen, his wife gave me a look, as if to say 'Good for you.'

I had arrived at 7.30 p.m. When I left the house at

10.30 p.m., with the labrador lying contentedly on the floor, the atmosphere had changed completely. The jacket and tie had been discarded and he'd had a few extra nips of whisky. As I made my way to the hallway once more, he shook me firmly by the hand. There was a genuine warmth in his words.

'You've got something, lady,' he smiled. 'You stay with it.'

Having come through such an experience, there was only one answer.

'Don't you worry, I will,' I said as I headed through the door. 'I will.'

The sad truth, however, was that I wasn't always going to overcome such dyed-in-the-wool attitudes. Not every-one had the open-mindedness to see things from a different perspective. The young Winterton man I dealt with around this time certainly didn't.

It had been his wife who had called me. Like many of my earliest clients, she had been referred to me by a local vet, sympathetic to my ideas. She said their dog, a Stafford-shire bull terrier, was very aggressive and had snapped at and bitten both her and her husband.

The root of their problems seemed to lie in the 'training classes' the husband had begun attending. Some of these classes are admirable, and I support them wholeheartedly. Some, however, make me wonder whether I'm inhabiting the same planet as other trainers. It seemed he'd been going to one of these.

The dog was, unsurprisingly given its breed, a pug-nacious character at times. The owner had been taught to grab it by the scruff of the neck. Every time he did this, however, the dog bit him. A vicious circle of violence was building between the two.

To say he was unreceptive to my ideas would be an understatement.

'There are people round here who think you're dangerous,' he said by way of introduction. 'They say you don't know what you're talking about.'

When I began to outline my ideas, he was hostile. 'I like my dog this way,' he said. 'I don't want to change him.'

I was determined to make my case and began laying out my argument for a change of tactics, and a more compassionate approach to training his dog. 'I'm just asking you to try something different,' I said to him.

It was clear I wasn't going to get very far. He simply challenged everything I said. 'How can I be sure of that?' he would ask. 'How do you know what the dog's thinking? What makes you more qualified to train him than me?'

It was still early days for me. In truth, I hadn't learned to express my ideas as forcibly or as coherently as I do today. I welcomed debate and discussion with people. But at the time I lacked confidence and felt intimidated by those who disagreed violently with the message I was imparting.

It was so frustrating. I felt out of my depth. What was particularly upsetting was that the wife was so desperate to help the dog – and her husband.

About a week after I visited them, she rang me to say things had deteriorated. I could feel the desperation building within her. She had tried applying my method and had found it worked. But when the husband had gone to pull the dog by its collar once more, it had taken a huge chunk out of his hand. The wound was so severe, he had needed stitches.

I could see that this situation was going to get worse, rather than better. For the next few nights I thought a lot about how I could get my message across to the husband. Different tactics and turns of phrase went round in my head.

Sadly I didn't get the opportunity to put any of them into practice, however. A few weeks after I spoke to his wife, I was talking to a neighbour who knew the couple and they came up in conversation.

'Oh, haven't you heard?' the neighbour said. 'He went for the husband last week, really badly this time. They had him put down that day.'

For all the progress I had made, it was one of the low points of that period.

I knew I could not allow myself to feel personally responsible for every dog I came across. I knew that I would have to face failure in some, perhaps many cases. It did not make things any easier, however. The learning curve was steep, but that was the hardest lesson of all.

Chapter 27

'A Little Under the Weather'

By the summer of 1998, my radio work was blossoming in unexpected ways. The phone-ins were going well. On the back of that success, the producers at BBC Radio Humberside asked me whether I'd be interested in doing a little reporting as well.

My first assignment took me to familiar ground – Cruft's. I recorded a diary of a day at the show in Olympia, chatting to as many of the colourful characters as I could point a microphone at. It felt odd not to be there competing, but I really enjoyed becoming a newshound once more. Back at the station the bosses were sufficiently pleased to ask me to do a longer piece, a one-to-one interview with – of all people – Monty Roberts. I travelled to another of his demonstrations, this time at Market Rasen. Again it was strange being so formal with someone whom I had now come to hold in such great affection and respect. And I was slightly thrown when it emerged that Monty not only knew about my work in adapting his method to dogs, but was complimentary about it as well. But I concentrated on my new, professional duties and got what I thought was a good interview out of Monty. Again, the powers-that-be back at Radio Humberside were pleased with the results.

By far my biggest assignment that year, however, was covering the Lincolnshire Show. Of all the county's shows, this was the biggest and the most important. It took place at a dedicated showground outside Lincoln and always attracted people in their thousands.

My job was to accompany Blair Jacobs, the station's DJ at the show, as he wandered around the huge site in the radio van. Blair was a big bear of a man, with an infectious laugh and a sociable nature that everyone warmed to. We enjoyed each other's company and worked well together. Much as I'd done at Cruft's, I would interview people and present assorted items on the interesting stories and personalities I came across. It was all good fun.

That summer's show took place on a scaldingly hot day. The temperature must have been in the nineties. By the end of the afternoon, when Blair and I had finished our broadcast, we were both red-faced and wilting.

'Come on, Jan, I think we deserve a drink,' Blair said. 'I know just the place.'

In the midst of the tented village was a marquee with a BBC sign on it. 'This is where all the bigwigs hang out,' Blair told me. 'Here's your chance to do a bit of networking.'

The tent was, I suppose, the nearest thing the Lincolnshire Show had to a VIP area. It was where people from the regional media gathered, including the bosses who were there that day.

The effort of running around the showground had taken its toll on me. I was absolutely drained and dying for a drink. The tent was invitingly laid out with tables full of prepared drinks. I grabbed a glass of orange juice and dispatched it all in one gulp. It hardly touched the sides. I was so thirsty I picked up a second one and was halfway through that when Blair reappeared at my side.

'Gosh, you're not wasting any time,' Blair smiled. 'Better be careful with those Bucks Fizzes, Jan. They pack a deceptive punch.'

'It's only orange juice,' I said.

'No it's not,' Blair replied, taking a sip. 'That's definitely Bucks Fizz.'

It was soon obvious that he was right.

My tolerance to drink had, if anything, deteriorated over the years. The fact that I was dehydrated as well only speeded things up. Within a few moments I felt woozy.

With the show's main events now drawing to a close, the tent was beginning to fill up. A group of serious-looking men in suits were gathering at the bar.

'That's the top brass from BBC Lincolnshire,' Blair told me. I could hardly take it in. 'You OK, Jan?' he asked, obviously spotting me wobbling.

'Not really,' I said.

By now the world was spinning. Fortunately Blair put his arm around me before I could keel over completely. There were a few chairs in the corner near the bar and he led me over towards it. As we passed the gathered executives, he nodded at me and said: 'She's a bit under the weather, I think it's the heat.' He got me safely to the chairs where he set me down gently.

Blair, bless him, saw how bad I was and realized I needed some fresh air. 'Just off to see what else is happening,' he said to one of his colleagues as he slipped me out of the tent back into the late afternoon air.

Goodness knows what would have happened to me if Blair hadn't been there. But he guided me safely to the radio van. He got me some food and I was soon feeling better.

By early evening I'd regained my composure. I was even feeling recovered enough to join Blair back in the VIP tent, where I met some of the senior figures again. One or two of them asked me whether I was feeling all right. 'We're obviously working you too hard, Jan,' one smiled. The atmosphere was lively and jolly, largely, I'm sure, because of the drink that was by now flowing freely.

I stuck to water this time, making sure to sniff each glass carefully before placing it to my lips.

Chapter 28

Pets Behaving Badly

As the winter of 1998 gave way to spring and the first, brilliant yellow flecks of daffodils began to dot the Lincolnshire landscape, the world really did seem as if it was starting afresh. For the umpteenth time I looked at my copy of the local paper and the small classified advert that was going to make – or break – my new life. It read:

PETS BEHAVING BADLY
The kind way to change undesirable
behaviour in your dog.

It had been more than two years since that first, furtive visit to Barrow-on-Humber and Pepsi. In the months after that memorable night, I'd developed my ideas a lot. I'd begun making more and more calls to friends and colleagues. My reputation had begun spreading purely by word of mouth, often through local vets, many of whom were generous and supportive of me.

It had been another encounter with the man who first gave me my inspiration that made my mind up. Monty

Roberts had returned to the UK and was staging another of his eye-popping demonstrations, this time at an arena at Grantham in Lincolnshire. I was still in awe of him and went along to the show with Wendy Broughton. By now I had been fortunate enough to meet Monty, and his support and interest had proven a huge inspiration for me to progress my ideas further.

After the show I found myself in a group of people that included Monty and one of his British protégés, Richard Maxwell. I had seen 'Max', as everyone knew him, on the television show *Pet Rescue* dealing with problem horses and admired his gentle, philosophical manner. Monty introduced us and we started talking.

'So I hear you do what Monty does, but with dogs. Does it work?' he wondered.

I nodded modestly and answered: 'It seems to.'

'So you must be doing this full time then?'

'Well, I'm getting a lot of requests, but I've got a job and a pension scheme and a house to run. It would be a big gamble to throw all that in. I can't decide what to do.'

He gave me a long smile. And it was then that he said something I'll never forget. 'Where's your choice?' he said. 'You either go with your head or you go with your heart. If you go with your head you won't be happy. If you go with your heart you will. You can't keep this thing to yourself.'

As I stood there taking in what he had said, he was called away. As he went he smiled at me again. 'Where's your choice?' he said once more as he waved goodbye.

On the way home, my mind was in overdrive. I had struggled financially all my life. But I was also at a crossroads. I was single. Both my children were now grown up and working. I had lost both my parents. In many ways there was nothing holding me back. I was in my forties and aware that time waits for no one.

The following week I walked into my boss's office, slipped my letter of resignation into his in-tray – and left it there. I had been in such a tizzy about the step I was taking that I had already removed it from the tray once. After three days carrying the letter around with me, it was looking decidedly creased and careworn. Finally, however, I had made my mind up. This was the moment. I was going for it – whatever the consequences.

With the money I had saved up I bought myself a van with a sliding door at the side and enough space to fit a couple of cages inside. I had a sticker made and fixed it to the back window. It read: 'Pets Behaving Badly: A Kind Way To Change Undesirable Behaviour'. I must admit it felt very strange when I wrote off to the Inland Revenue, telling them that I was starting a business. But the strangeness didn't last long.

The response to the adverts I put in the *Hull Daily Mail* and the *Scunthorpe & Grimsby Telegraph* was slow. At first I received more replies to another advert I placed, for the Smart Dogs Grooming Service. After a couple of days, however, the phone rang and a voice at the other end of the line asked: 'Is that Pets Behaving Badly?'

'Yes, it is. How can I help?' I replied.

'It's our boxer,' the voice began, before coming out with a phrase I've heard hundreds, if not thousands of times since. 'We love him to pieces, but . . .'

The feeling that I was making a new beginning was

unmistakable as I arrived at a Grimsby housing estate the following day, a Saturday.

The estate must have been completed only weeks, perhaps even days, earlier. The neatly arranged, redbrick houses gleamed so brightly, I wondered whether I'd arrived accidentally at Legoland. The roads, the pavements, the newly potted plants; everything was pristine. As I climbed out of the car I could almost smell the drying paintwork.

Things were just as immaculate inside the home of my first professional clients, a couple in their twenties.

They had been married for a couple of years but this was their first home together and they were evidently as proud as Punch to be living there. For the wife, in particular, it was clearly her dream home. The house – and her neatly manicured garden – were flawless. Dust did not settle here for more than seconds. It would have been a brave weed that had stuck its head up in her rose garden.

The only blot on the landscape was their dog, a particularly manic two-year-old boxer called Flash. The moment I walked in it was obvious why they believed he was hell bent on turning their dream home into a house of horrors.

Flash was well named. He bounded around at lightning speed. To me again it was clear he was incredibly stressed. By now, though, I'd learned from my early experiences and gone in with a plan. So I began by completely ignoring Flash and asking his owners to do precisely the same.

We needed an area to which Flash could be removed when he misbehaved. The wife didn't want to use the bedroom. She was terrified he might scratch her new doors. So we agreed to put him out into the garden.

Unfortunately, by now a light rain had begun to fall.

Flash was a ball of energy, a real handful, and kept jumping up at his owners. Whenever he did this I asked the husband to lead him outside by the collar, then shut the door. I remember the first time we put him out, Flash was bouncing around like crazy in the garden. His head would appear in the upper half of the window, like something out of a *Tom & Jerry* cartoon.

When the time came to let him back in, his paws were covered in a light film of grass and mud. Far from ignoring him, the couple fussed around him cleaning him up. This, of course, was a bad idea – but they were insistent he couldn't run around with muddy paws.

I'm sure this contributed to the slowness of the process. People have to be 100 per cent focused on my method in these crucial early stages and the wife in particular was just as concerned about the state of her carpet. Nevertheless I was determined to persevere.

Each time Flash misbehaved badly he was ejected from the house. Each time he went out, it seemed the rain was coming down even harder. And each time he reappeared his paws seemed to have picked up more mess. The spotless light green carpet was being transformed into a brownish, mud-spattered mess. What's more, by now Flash had also managed to smear mud on assorted pieces of furniture.

I was trying to remain relaxed and in control but inwardly I was panicking. Fortunately, salvation was close at hand – and it was Flash who provided it. I have always believed that dogs are in many ways brighter than us. It is one of the reasons I love them so much. Over the years I have seen many dogs display more common sense than their owners – and so it proved with Flash.

In my mind, there was no doubt that Flash had cottoned on to what was happening. After we'd ejected him for about the tenth time he proved how well he understood. He had been back in the house for a few minutes and had behaved perfectly. Suddenly he couldn't help himself and jumped up at a noise. Even before I or his owner could make a move towards him, he was heading back towards the open door to the garden and out again.

He knew the score and was saving us all the time and trouble. It was as if he was saying, 'Look, I get what's going on here, can we move along a little more quickly before everyone gets too upset.'

At that moment all three of us looked at each other and burst out laughing. It was relief more than anything else. And it had been Flash who defused the situation. That proved the turning point of the day. Soon afterwards, Flash came back in from the garden, headed for his favourite spot and lay down quietly. He remained indoors, safe from the rain, for the rest of my time there. His owners spent the evening, no doubt, with a Hoover and a gallon of detergent to hand.

I don't think I've been so relieved in my entire life. And to my delight, the behaviour continued to improve in the days and weeks that followed.

Every experience I had during those early days was a valuable one. But the memory of my first professional job still reminds me of a fundamental truth.

It had been by listening to my own dogs that I had seen the behaviour that led me to my method. That rainy afternoon, Flash had shown me that in my new venture, I would have to watch what each and every dog was telling me. If I was going to be successful, I had to allow the dogs to guide me to the solutions.

Chapter 29

Restoration Work

During those days as an apprentice 'dog listener', nothing gave me as much pleasure as dealing with rescue dogs. With Barmie, I'd experienced the joy of seeing a damaged and discarded dog transformed at first hand. But each time I visited an owner in a similar situation, I found myself somehow trying just that little bit harder. The rewards were often wonderful.

Two dogs in particular spring to mind, for very different reasons.

In many ways working with rescue dogs reminded me of my experience of working with people with severe learning disabilities in Brigg. They couldn't be pushed too fast – as I'd found myself with Barmie.

This was certainly the case with Scud, a dog that lived with its owner Vanessa near Oxford.

He had got his name soon after arriving at his owner Vanessa's home, a lovely cottage in a small village near the city. He shot around the house with all the speed and destructive power of a Scud missile.

Scuddy's problems were perfectly understandable. Vanessa had found him at Battersea Dogs' Home in London. He was a rescue dog, and had been severely damaged by some trauma in his past. The hardest thing with rescue dogs was not knowing what the root cause of their problems were. We didn't know what had happened to Scud, what ghosts haunted him. All we could do was treat him as well as we could – and hope he came to trust us for doing so.

Vanessa had applied my method well. But she had over-ridden one crucial piece of advice. One thing I was already stressing to people was that they had to keep their dog within the home environment for at least a week, maybe a fortnight while they underwent the training. This was partly based on my own experience and partly based on common sense. Dogs are not robots, they are flesh and blood too. I knew that it took time for the method to really sink in. And that they could not be removed from the home environment until they were really ready for it.

Vanessa hadn't been able to resist taking Scud out for a walk during the early days. Predictably, he had reverted to his old high octane self. It wasn't the last time I'd have this conversation. I told her that she had not only tried to run before she could walk, she'd actually tried to walk before she could walk. She had to be more patient. She had to give the method more time.

It wasn't very long afterwards that I received a postcard from Vanessa. In it she described the moment when she knew. She was aware the biggest test was going to come when Scuddy was faced with a rabbit, a duck or a moorhen during his morning walk. In fact it was a coot that he saw in the open space before him. He took off like the heat-seeking missile of old.

Vanessa called him in an effort to stop him attacking the bird. He instantly stopped, turned and ran back to her, as she put it, 'like an arrow'.

A neighbour happened to be out walking nearby and witnessed the scene. As she and Vanessa chatted later, the neighbour commented on the beautifully trained dog she had seen in the fields. 'Whatever happened to that one you got from Battersea Dogs' Home?' she wondered.

I remember for different reasons another rescue dog I dealt with around this time.

His owner had called one autumn evening and had been nothing if not intriguing. He was a well-spoken gentleman who wanted help with the springer spaniel he had taken in, again from Battersea Dogs' Home.

I knew I was getting somewhere when people said to me: 'I've got something that'll sort you out,' and then went on to outline a problem I'd already dealt with a dozen times or more. Sure enough, the problems the man described were nowhere near as unusual as he imagined them to be. Even from the phone call I guessed that the springer was excitable because he suffered from separation anxiety. What was unusual at the time was the client's request that I treat the details of my visit and his address in complete confidence.

I was intrigued, and travelled to his home in a beautiful cathedral city in the north with all sorts of ideas going through my head. None of them was anywhere near the mark, as it turned out.

As I walked into the man's lovely home, it was as if I was stepping into some strange, fantastical museum. Suddenly I was surrounded by historic mechanical musical instruments, barrel organs, clockwork fairground orchestras and hurdy-gurdies.

He told me that he specialized in restoring the instruments and that many had been recovered from rubbish dumps or scrapyards. The house was full of instruments, many of them probably priceless, if not in financial terms then certainly in terms of their historical importance. They were some of the most beautiful pieces of craftsmanship I'd ever seen. No wonder he'd been so concerned that I should promise not to talk about the contents of his home.

As I guessed, their dog was suffering from separation anxiety. He became very agitated and made a mess in the house when the couple were away. (Not, thankfully, in the rooms where the instruments were kept.) Using my normal method, I was able to alleviate this problem quite quickly, in two or three hours or so.

To me, the transformations I was achieving were becoming more commonplace. They were always wonderful to behold, but I was perhaps less surprised when I saw them. The couple, on the other hand, were ecstatic at the change I achieved. They'd never seen the dog looking so relaxed.

As we had a cup of tea afterwards, the husband asked me if I would like to see his workshop. I jumped at the opportunity, I must say. My working life had become hugely fulfilling in itself. But by now I was also getting to meet a wonderful variety of people. Talking to him afterwards I was fascinated by his work, and touched by his passion for the beautiful works of art in his house.

What impressed me most, however, was his uncompromising attitude to his work. He believed in the inherent beauty of these instruments and saw it as his mission to restore them to their original state. He refused to cut corners or use modern methods. He had acquired the right woods, the right resins, the right veneers, the right paints. He used tools that were of the right period. He had a library bulging with books on the history of these instruments and the men who had made them back in the eighteenth and nineteenth centuries.

'When these things come in here they have been discarded. People have given up on them,' he said. 'I take them off the scrap heap, I strip them down to their basic parts and I put them together again so that they are as new.'

I was riveted listening to him. Throughout I just nodded.

I think he was enjoying showing me around. I sensed he and his wife didn't have many visitors. Then after a while he stopped and smiled. 'What am I talking about, of course you know. This is what you do,' he said.

I didn't quite know what he meant, but before I could speak he went on. 'You take dogs, like my springer, poor creatures that have been tossed on to the scrap heap by people who don't care, and restore them by stripping them down to their basic instincts. You've seen the beauty in them and made them whole again,' he said.

Sometimes the most powerful moments arrive in the most understated and unexpected ways. I had never thought of my work in that way. Nor would I ever, probably, unless I'd met this eloquent stranger. It was another small but significant moment. Not so long ago I'd doubted whether I should even be interfering in the lives of other people's animals. Now I felt assured that I was doing some good.

Throughout those early years, I'd always struggled to find a way of describing myself. 'So now I'm a dog restorer,' I smiled to myself on the drive home. 'I can live with that.'

Chapter 30

'It's Making a Fool of Me'

The Winterton Show was less than a month away and Pete was in a terrible state.

Our paths had crossed again at the stables one morning and I'd immediately noticed something different about his demeanour. He didn't even seem interested in tutting and shaking his head at me, normally one of the highlights of his day.

To be honest, I knew from others around the village that he wasn't such a bad old sort at heart. I felt a touch sorry for him so I bit the bullet.

'What's wrong with you? You look about as happy as a bulldog that's just swallowed a wasp.'

The attempt at humour was lost on him. He growled and carried on pitching his fork into his delivery of hay. After a few moments, however, he came over to me. He was clearly in need of someone to share his problems with.

'It's my show beast,' he grunted in reply. 'It's making a blasted fool of me.'

Pete was well known locally for the quality of the cattle he bred. He often won prizes at the show. He told me he'd had high hopes for his best young Lincolnshire Red steer that year. But the bullock had proven a nightmare on the training ground.

'It's no good, he's carting me all over the place when I try to show him,' he said.

Doing well at the show each July was of huge importance to farmers like Pete. It was a matter of professional and personal pride to them. It was, in some ways, how they measured themselves as members of the community – and definitely how the rest of the community judged them.

Since our early run-ins, Pete had shown no signs of accepting my ideas. But I still found myself wondering whether, somehow, I might be able to help him.

'Look, Pete, I know you'll probably think it's a pile of old rubbish, but there might be something I could suggest to improve things,' I said. It was a sign of how desperate he was that he even allowed me to carry on. To my amazement, he invited me to his farm the following day.

I arrived to find him in the field with one of his steers. It was, I have to admit, a lovely-looking beast. Pete had bred well. The ox's coat was gleaming. It looked in rude health. But it was clear it had a mind of its own.

Pete was attempting to train the steer so that it 'worked well' in the competition ring on show day. Basically he wanted the steer to walk in and out of the ring, stand semi still for a moment or two while the judges assessed it and then leave without causing a commotion. It may not have seemed a particularly tall order – but it was proving nigh on impossible for poor Pete.

When I arrived he held a short length of rope attached to a head collar and was trying to lead the steer on a short walk. The animal showed no interest and was twisting and turning in every direction except the one Pete wanted it to move. Each time it did this, Pete let loose a four-letter word or two and gave a yank on the rope. His frustration was clear to see. So too was one of the reasons why he was getting nowhere.

I had, by this time, watched Monty Roberts at work in his famous round pen perhaps half a dozen times. I understood his ideas and his 'join up' method and had headed to Pete's with the idea of adapting them to the steer.

I couldn't fail to be struck by the irony of the situation. Pete had regularly had a go at me for my belief in Monty's method. Now here he was, ready to put it into practice.

'You can't treat a dog the same way you treat a horse,' he had scoffed once. In this respect he was right. And he was right again when he said I couldn't treat his steer the same way I did dogs. Of course not, they couldn't speak the same language. The point was that they did speak a language, and that the key to gaining greater control over their behaviour was in understanding that language.

I explained to Pete that the first thing he had to do was win the bullock's trust. From there, he would be able to establish leadership. The best way to do this, I told him, was by exuding an air of calm and control – not by shouting and indulging in a tug-of-war contest.

So we began by calming the situation down. I helped Pete to carry out a simple drill in which he approached and then walked away from the steer. The idea was that it would come to trust him and eventually move towards him whenever he walked away. Pete was a little flustered to begin with. One of my mantras when working with dog owners was: 'Keep the pulse rate low.' When I shared this with Pete he gave me one of his old-fashioned looks. Inwardly, I'm sure he was thinking 'Stupid woman' once more. Outwardly, however, he played along.

The steer had been in a pretty intense state when I arrived. After about ten or fifteen minutes of this new approach, however, it had become much calmer. I now got Pete to move in even closer to the animal and to reward it with a few reassuring strokes to the back of its neck. (This is a hugely symbolic act for all animals. The back of the neck is their most vulnerable area. By touching this area a human is signalling friendship. In return, by allowing them to do so, an animal is signalling a huge degree of trust.) The steer responded well to this so I now encouraged Pete to gently take the lead – only taking a step or two before coming to rest and waiting calmly and peacefully for a few minutes each time.

He didn't say much. He was a man of action, not words. But by then he didn't need to tell me what he was thinking. I could see he was pleased with the progress we'd made.

As I left him there it was late afternoon. I guessed he'd be in the field working the steer until long after milking time that night.

That year the Winterton Show took place under a sky so flawlessly blue you couldn't help but stop and simply stare at it from time to time.

The perfection of the day brought out a bigger crowd than usual. The main competition arena, the arts and crafts marquees and – of course – the beer tent seemed to be alive with locals intent on enjoying a big day out.

I'd been involved in the show for several years by now. But after my early adventures with the Pony Club and the cross-country course, I'd given the horses a wide berth and concentrated instead on the relative calm and order of the dog show. I'd become one of the judges and – for all the competitiveness and occasional tension – found it fun and rewarding.

This year, as usual, I'd arrived nice and early to have a look around. As I did so I'd watched the rest of the show taking shape around me. I'd seen the horseboxes and cattle trucks drifting in all morning, the mini-village of marquees and tents being raised up. Among the arrivals I'd noticed Pete's lorry. Later on I saw him sponging down his steer and making all the last-minute nips and tucks to its tail, hooves and horns. In the bright sunshine the ox looked absolutely magnificent. 'But will it behave?' I wondered to myself.

By mid-morning I was in the thick of the action with the dog show. I was not so wrapped up, however, that I couldn't hear the sound of the Tannoy summoning the latest entrants to the main showring. 'Would owners of steers, two years or less, please make their way with their animals to the main show arena,' the rather plummy voice said. For some strange reason, I was suddenly aware I had butterflies in my stomach.

There was no way I could escape to watch him. And soon I was distracted by events in my own arena. It must have been at least an hour or two later, as I took a tea break, that I saw Pete making his way across the meadows towards me. He was clutching a rosette and was beaming from ear to ear.

'Just popped over to show you this,' he said, removing his ever-present cap and showing me the rosette. 'The little lad did good,' he went on. 'He got a good second.'

He was clearly as pleased as Punch. I'd never seen him so talkative. He spent ten minutes explaining how he'd coached the steer to walk quietly to a stop then to remain there while a stranger poked and prodded at him. Back at his farm he'd enlisted all sorts of helpers to act as make-believe judges in the run-up to the big day. Even the post-man had been dragooned into helping one morning.

'So perhaps you're on to something after all, Jan,' he said as his excitement finally waned. And he was still smiling when he headed off again, no doubt for a celebratory pint or two in the beer tent.

Somehow, I doubted either my name or that of Monty Roberts would come up in the ale-fuelled version of events he was about to unfurl for the gathered farming folk. But to be honest I didn't mind one bit. I'd had some memorable moments during those early days. But nothing quite as satisfying as that one.

Chapter 31

Law and Order

Within a few months of setting up in business, I was working flat out. I got to see more of the north than I'd ever seen before. I could have worked for the AA, so detailed was my knowledge of the highways and byways of Lincolnshire, Yorkshire and beyond. It was rewarding, if at times exhausting work.

With the business shaping up to be a success, I decided it was time to pay attention to my social life. And for me that meant once more trying to get myself back into the show world.

Once more the idea of breeding show-winning English springer spaniels had begun to bubble away in my mind. During my first foray into 'dogdom' as we liked to call it, I had been friendly with a couple called Frances and Bob Jackson. The Jacksons were – and remain – very well known within the dog fraternity as the premier breeders of English springer spaniels. I gave them a call, registering my interest in taking a puppy from them. Soon afterwards I got a call back from Frances, asking me to visit them at their home in Eyam, near Sheffield. I called the beautiful puppy I collected that day Molly.

Molly quickly settled into life at home with the rest of the pack, which had by now been extended further by the arrival of Sadie, Sasha's daughter. The arrival of a new dog had proven a problem in the past. Now I was able to integrate newcomers more easily and painlessly by applying my method. I was so pleased with the way Molly fitted in with the rest of the gang that I was soon back on the phone to the Jacksons.

It wasn't long afterwards that I was on the road to Eyam again to collect another puppy, which I named Spike Milligan after my comic hero.

I had taken Molly with the specific intention of showing her – and then probably breeding from her as well. I was itching to get back out into the competitive world again, I must admit. It didn't take long for Molly to start being successful. In fact, aged six months she was first in her class at the first show she ever entered. It would be the beginning of a run of many rosettes.

As ever, it was about much more than the competition. It was great to meet up with old faces from the past. I didn't raise the subject of what I was up to unless asked directly. Apart from anything else, most show people consider themselves – quite correctly – dog experts in their own right. I wasn't going to shout the odds in their company. I enjoyed the social side of it too much to risk offending or upsetting anyone with my ideas.

Showing and show people were now a more important release than ever for me. Wherever I travelled I knew I would be surrounded by people who genuinely cared about their dogs and who were prepared to do almost anything to maintain their welfare. As my work developed and I began to get involved in the darker side of man's relationship with his so-called best friend, their company became more and more precious to me.

Since the distant days of my childhood I'd borne a deep-rooted anger at man's cruelty to dogs. I still feel horror at the memory of my uncle's dog Bruce being mentally taunted and tortured in their kitchen in Fulham. I remain adamantly opposed to some of the violent training methods used in the gundog world, in particular.

The more I succeeded with a non-violent approach to training, the more incensed I had become. To my mind, no one needs to resort to physical force to get a dog to behave well. So when I read newspaper reports about a trio of police dog trainers who had been found guilty of abusing a German shepherd I felt almost physically sick. I also felt a personal responsibility to do something about it. My reaction set off a chain of events that I could never have predicted.

The story made national headlines both in the newspapers and on television. The men, a handler and two trainers, had been working for the Essex Constabulary. The dog, a German shepherd, had not been responding to their training so the trio resorted to violence. During my years living in the countryside and working at the sanctuary, I'd heard some awful stories. But this went beyond anything I'd encountered. According to the reports, they had first of all tied the dog's collar and lead to the upper part of its cage so that he was effectively hanging by the neck. He was left there with his legs dangling, thrashing around. After a while they let him loose while keeping him on a tight lead, expecting him to have learned a lesson. Anyone with a smidgeon of sense would know that the dog had only one option in this situation. He couldn't freeze, he couldn't flee, he had to fight. But as the dog became more aggressive so too did the men. They beat, kicked and punched it into submission. Apparently the dog was left in its cage for a long while before anyone thought to give it medical attention. No one could have been surprised when it later died from the grievous wounds these thugs had inflicted on it.

At this stage the three officers had been suspended from duty pending an inquiry. They would eventually be found guilty and discharged from the force, but I didn't know this at the time.

I can remember shaking with rage when I read the report. I was angry not just at what they'd done but at the relative lightness of their punishment. OK, they'd lost their jobs and perhaps their pension rights. But compared to what the dog had suffered that was nothing.

I've never been a member of the 'green ink brigade', as Ted and Nora used to call the regular, slightly deranged letter writers who used to drop their weekly rants off at the *Lincolnshire Times*. The last time I'd been so moved by injustice was when the Water Board allowed us to get flooded out in Firsby. This was far more serious, to my mind. I fired off a letter to the most senior policeman I could think of, the Commissioner of the Metropolitan Police. A week or so later I received what looked like a standard letter in reply.

It said something along the lines of 'This is not normal procedure and we can assure you we treat our dogs with the utmost respect'. This seemed so inadequate I found myself sending off a second letter, basically saying I didn't find their promise very reassuring at all.

I can't remember exactly what I wrote. What I do recall, however, is that I was soon opening a second reply from the Met, this time inviting me to come and reassure myself. The invitation was to visit the Metropolitan Police Dog Training Centre in Keston near Bromley, south of London.

The week I received the letter I was doing my regular phone-in on Radio Humberside. Towards the end of the show, as usual, the DJ, Paul Teage, asked me, 'So what else is new, Jan?' I mentioned the letters I'd written and the subsequent invitation and told him how much I was looking forward to seeing what they did at the Met Training Centre. I promised to report back on what I found there.

As I was leaving the studio one of the news guys grabbed me and asked whether I'd do a piece for him. 'It's a good story that, Jan,' he said.

It went out on the air the following day. The first phone call I received in response to the broadcast was from the *Mail on Sunday* in London. They had been tipped off about what I'd said on Radio Humberside and wanted to know more. Never one to edit myself, I vented my anger at the Essex Constabulary and explained the sequence of events that had followed my letter to the Met.

Perhaps it was naiveté on my part, but I was mortified at the way the story came out in the paper the following

Sunday. Essentially it said that, in the light of the Essex case, I'd been called in to show the police dog handlers how to do their job.

'Great,' I thought to myself, 'they are really going to roll out the red carpet for me now.'

It was my first taste of national publicity and the momentum it produced was amazing. Before I had taken in the full significance of the *Mail on Sunday* piece, its sister paper the *Daily Mail* had called me up.

'We're interested to know what exactly you do,' the journalist explained. I related the basics of my method and how I liked to work. They asked me whether I'd be willing to do a demonstration for them. The results would form the basis for an article in their Weekend magazine.

Before I knew it I was travelling to Reading to work with a couple of dogs selected by the *Mail*. The visit went really well, as did the interview. I couldn't feel pleased with myself for long, however. I'd arranged with the Met to drive down to Keston on the following day.

I'd called them to finalize the details of my visit after the *Mail on Sunday* piece had been published. The response had been very direct, businesslike. 'We'll see you then, Miss Fennell,' said the voice at the end of the line. It wasn't paranoia on my part. There was clearly a coolness that must have been related to the newspaper piece.

I drove down to Keston with two of my dogs, Chaser and Sadie. The welcome was every bit as frosty as I'd expected it to be.

I was greeted by a sergeant, Steve Golding. He was very upright and formal, clearly wary of this supposed expert who was there to put him straight on his job. His answers were confined to clipped 'yeses' and 'nos'. I felt as welcome as a wart.

I knew my job was to allay their fears. As he gave me the official guided tour around the museum, we discovered a shared love of springers. I was careful not to say anything that might be deemed too controversial or radical. These were serious, dedicated, professional dog handlers and trainers. And clearly the Essex trio were bad apples.

Steve Golding and I got on sufficiently well for him to invite me to the café for a cup of coffee. I walked in to discover at least thirty police officers in there. Every single one of them turned and stared at me as I walked in. I smiled the friendliest smile I could muster and kept my head down.

Steve arranged for me to spend some time with a trainer, Eric Dench. He showed me a demonstration in which a German shepherd was being trained in the art of 'bringing down' a man. It was Eric who finally eased my nerves. 'You're not the big-head you were made out to be then,' he said.

At no point that day did I try and offer my method as an alternative. I knew it would have been completely out of order. The school had been training dogs far longer than I had. They had their method and in 99.9 per cent of cases it was applied rigorously and properly. I came away feeling the utmost respect for the job they do.

I departed with two thoughts. First, I would be able to allay the fears of the radio listeners who were worried that the Essex case represented the tip of a brutal iceberg. It didn't. Nothing could have been further from the truth, in fact. But I'd also been taken seriously by some of the most respected dog people in Britain. It felt like another step forward.

It was in the weeks afterwards that the full significance of that step slowly revealed itself.

I don't know whether the police grapevine came into operation. But soon I was being invited to visit another police dog trainer, this time attached to the West Midlands force. Now I was being asked to apply my method.

The trainer, Teresa, had a problem with her German shepherd, Mac. I had watched the routine that was causing her difficulties when I visited the Met training centre. Police dogs are trained to 'bring down' criminals by officers wearing coats with specially padded sleeves. Mac was a tenacious dog – a little too tenacious, in fact. The first time Mac had been asked to go through the routine he had refused to let go, even when the exercise was over. 'The officer in the padded sleeve wasn't very happy about it,' Teresa told me with a half smile. 'By the end he was shouting "Get this damned dog off me".'

Obviously this would be no laughing matter out on the streets where Mac was going to be working mainly as a sniffer dog. In fact, if he did the same thing in the real world the consequences for him might be catastrophic.

While the approach was official, the officer who called me made it clear that this was something of a last resort. I was left in no doubt that a large percentage of his colleagues thought my method was a load of bunkum. But they were prepared to give it a go.

Teresa lived in Gloucester. I travelled down and spent some time with her. I was delighted a few weeks later when I heard that Mac had passed out of the training school and was a working member of the West Midlands Constabulary.

I couldn't quite believe the way the establishment was opening itself up to me in this way. Around this time too I was asked to help a guide dog for the first time. To my mind, there are no finer group of dog trainers in this country than the men and women who produce these extraordinary animals. To be asked to work with them left me feeling a little bit humble, I must admit. The dog I was asked to help was a labrador based in Halifax. It was living with its blind owner and working well with him. But when it was off duty, spending time with the rest of his family, it was getting into trouble. I had decided in advance that my training would need to complement rather than contradict or contravene that which the dog had received through the Guide Dog for the Blind Association. So I concentrated on working with the rest of the family while the dog was off duty. I was able to improve its behaviour significantly in the space of a few weeks.

We are all attached to our dogs, but for someone this animal was now a lifeline. It made me proud to think I'd helped a little in providing that lifeline.

Of all the cases that I dealt with during that period, however, by far the most significant came when I was called one day by a solicitor from Staffordshire.

'I don't know whether you'll be able to help, but I represent a family whose dog is the subject of a court destruction order,' he began.

He went on to explain that Hector, a Pyrenean mountain dog, had bitten a woman passer-by outside the family's home.

'The family are desperate,' he said. 'They think you're the dog's only chance.'

It breaks my heart to think about the number of dogs that are destroyed unnecessarily through the courts each year. I had, of course, been through a similarly hideous experience myself all those years ago with Purdey. But I wasn't going to commit myself to doing this unless I was sure of a few things. I needed to know whether the family were prepared to apply my method. And I had to meet Hector.

When I travelled down to Staffordshire it didn't take me long to answer both doubts positively. They were a lovely, loving family. And Hector was a good dog, if a little rambunctious. With patience, hard work and application, I was sure they had a chance at least of having the destruction order lifted.

I wrote a report to be presented to the court. It explained that Hector's problems had been diagnosed and that, with my help, the family were putting into effect a rehabilitation programme which should prevent a repeat of the attack ever happening.

I must admit I sweated over that letter more than any other I'd written in a long, long time. I sent if off to the solicitor who thanked me and said we'd given it our best shot.

'It's up to the magistrate now,' he said.

A day was fixed for the hearing. I got up that day having slept poorly the night before. Midway through the morning, the solicitor rang.

'Good news, Jan,' he said. 'The order has been changed to a controlling order. Provided Hector doesn't transgress again, he won't have to be destroyed.'

I must confess I cried my eyes out when I heard the news. They were tears of joy, of course. But they were tinged with sadness too. My mind, as it often did now, went back to Purdey and the terrible way her life was brought to a premature end. If only I'd known then what I knew now.

Chapter 32

New Horizons

It was a lovely autumnal afternoon and Wendy and I were taking a breather while out riding in the countryside around her farm. We'd been sitting there for a while, simply drinking in the peace and quiet, our thoughts interrupted only by an occasional burst of birdsong or a whinny from one of the gently grazing horses. Then out of the blue Wendy started giggling.

'What's wrong?' I asked her, genuinely perplexed.

'Who would have thought it? Who would ever have thought it?' she said, still tittering away.

'Thought what?'

'You.'

'Me? What are you talking about, Wendy?' I said, still lost at what was tickling her so much.

'Who would have thought you'd discover something no one else had? Who would have thought you'd be the one to come up with something that's going to revolutionize the way people train their dogs?'

I've never been any good at taking a compliment, so I

sat pretending to ignore her while fiddling with Raffie's saddle.

It didn't shut her up.

'We are so proud of you, you know, and you should be proud of yourself,' she said. 'You're doing something that you love and you're doing it well. Good for you.'

She knew I was quick to tears. I could feel myself welling up, I must admit. But fortunately the horses were getting restless. Wendy sensed how I was feeling and quickly defused the atmosphere. 'Come on,' she said. 'Race you across the field.'

I had been fortunate to have a number of important friends over the years, but there were few more influential than Wendy. As we raced across the open country, a gentle breeze in our hair, her words set me thinking once more.

There had been times in the past year or two when I'd found myself questioning what on earth I thought I was up to. At times like that I could hear my mother somewhere saying: 'Who the hell are you to be changing the way the world thinks?' By now, however, I was sure I was heading in the right direction. Out in the middle of nowhere on horseback that day, I thought to myself: 'Yes, why not, why shouldn't I feel proud of myself?'

As I thought about it I realized I was proud of several things, not just the success I was beginning to achieve. It was now twenty-five years since I'd left London for the country. There had been times when I'd doubted that I'd ever fit in. But now I knew I belonged in this landscape and in this life.

I hadn't been down to London more than a handful of times in the last ten years. It was mostly Cruft's or other dog events that took me there. Each time I visited I felt a strange conflict within me. I am – and always will be – a Londoner at heart. Being back there, particularly on the familiar turf of Fulham, was a warming experience, even though the place bore little resemblance to the community I had grown up in during the 1950s. Yet at the same time I always breathed a huge sigh of relief when I made it back to the open landscape of Lincolnshire. It felt like home too.

I was proud, as well, of having overcome the difficulties I'd faced. Financially and emotionally I was back on my feet after some dark and difficult times. The children were doing well, Ellie teaching in South Wales, Tony working locally in Lincolnshire and also enjoying himself as a musician in a local band. He'd even had a play that he'd written put on at the local theatre, the Plowright in Scunthorpe. Ellie and her long-time partner Matt had also revealed that they were about to make me a grandmother.

I had always felt that there was no point in regretting the past. Now I saw how wise that philosophy had been. Although there were things that I wished hadn't happened, I knew too that if things had happened differently I would not have been the same person. Emotionally I had come through a lot. Yet if I hadn't been through all the anger, pain and betrayal, I wouldn't have found myself being pushed in the direction I was. I wouldn't have found myself being able to help so many people – and to feel so good about myself in doing so.

As Raffie galloped through the verdant Lincolnshire landscape that afternoon, a million thoughts passed through my mind. For a moment I remembered my Great-Uncle

Jim. Since the distant days when I'd sat on Kitty's back with him in Battersea Park, my love affair with horses had deepened. Riding Raffie as I was now in the open countryside was one of the great pleasures in life. I loved the feeling of freedom it brought. But I loved too the sensation of working in harmony with a living, breathing animal. It had been good old Great-Uncle Jim and his tales of Buffalo Bill's circus that had first instilled the idea of man and animal working in harmony together. It had never left me. Now, riding Raffie, moving in concert with him, I saw how significant his words had been.

Everything that I knew to be wrong with traditional training had to do with the coercion it involved. Dogs were not being encouraged to do things of their own free will. They were being forced. I sensed that Great-Uncle Jim would have approved of what I was trying to do. He would, I'm sure, have appreciated that I was trying to go with the dog's nature, to listen to its instinctive language rather than imposing our own.

The more I thought about it, the more I felt I had to be proud about. After all the years of struggle and relying on other people, my work was giving me the opportunity to be in charge of my own destiny. That was as important to me as anything. My biggest nightmare had always been relying on or taking orders from someone who didn't know what they were talking about. I'd had to do it often enough. From my mother to the assorted bosses I'd encountered, I'd always felt that I'd been told what to do with my life. I could feel those days of powerlessness were drawing to a close.

One final idea stuck in my mind that day. Since my

earliest years living with my family, I had been doing the things that were expected of me: underachievement at school, marriage, children – a life of domesticity. The scary thing was that, for a long time, it was what I believed I was born to do. Now I really felt that by finding something that was unique, that no one else had done before, I had discovered my own uniqueness. There was a time when, once more, I would have heard my mother's voice in the background telling me off for talking this way. 'Listen to yourself, Janice,' she'd have said. But no longer. I had found myself, I felt I had found out why I was really here.

My last thought was of the dogs that had helped me to get to this juncture. I found myself thinking how lucky I'd been to have shared my life with so many wonderful characters. Shane, Lady and Khan, Sasha and Barmie, each of them hugely different dogs, but each of them the companion – and sometimes the guide – I needed at crucial times.

I had no idea what lay ahead. Of one thing, however, I was sure. It was, perhaps, the one thing about which I'd been certain since the earliest days of my childhood. Wherever I was headed, faithful friends like these would always be there with me.